School HAND BOOK for boys

2003 2004

Matt Parselle

BARDFIELD PRESS

PERSONAL INFORMATION

Full Name ....

Date of Birth ....

Address ....

....

....

....

....

Phone ....

E-mail ....

....

Height ....

Weight ....

FAVOURITE THINGS

Singer ....

Band ....

Actor/Actress ....

....

Film ....

....

TV programme ....

....

Sport ....

Team ....

Hobby ....

Book ....

School subject ....

Use this page to keep a record of any important dates, as well as all the birthdays of your family and friends.

IMPORTANT DATES

2003

August
26............Summer Bank Holiday

September
27............Jewish New Year

October
31............Hallowe'en

November
5..............Bonfire Night
11............Remembrance Day
30............St Andrew's Day

December
21............Winter Solstice
25............Christmas Day
26............Boxing Day

2004

January
1..............New Years Day
22............Chinese New Year

February
14............St Valentine's Day

March
1..............St David's Day
17............St Patrick's Day

April
9..............Good Friday
11............Easter Sunday
12............Easter Monday
23............St George's Day

May
3..............May Day Bank Holiday
31............Spring Bank Holiday

June
21............Summer Solstice

July
4..............Independence Day (USA)
14............Bastille Day (France)

BIRTHDAYS

January

February

March

April

May

June

July

August

September

October

November

December

School does have its good points. Honest!
You get to meet up with your mates, you get loads of holidays and, very occasionally, you learn something almost interesting. But school has its downsides, too, so here's some basic advice on what to do if things start to go wrong.

Beating bullies

Nobody likes being bullied.
Whether it involves name-calling or someone actually hitting you, bullying can make your life a misery. And why should you have to put up with it? Simple answer: you shouldn't, and you should tell someone (either your teacher or your parents) as soon as possible. Sadly, things aren't always as easy as that — perhaps the person you're telling won't take your problem seriously, or maybe you really can't bring yourself to tell anyone you know. If that sounds like you, then you could try calling Childline on 0800 1111 at any time of day or night for some free, and completely

private advice. Remember, bullies are cowards and rely on frightening people so much that they won't tell anyone. Don't let them win.

Work

With both schoolwork and homework, most people go through at least one stage where they feel they're getting left behind and everything is getting on top of them. At times like these, it's all too easy to put it off for another day and settle down in front of your PlayStation or the telly for an evening's solid lazing around. However, you can only avoid it for so long, so here are a few tips if you want to get all your work done and have a life!

1 **If you're finding things a bit tough, talk to your teacher about it.** They won't be angry if you don't understand the subject – they're there to support you, and should be all too happy to give you a little extra help.

2 **If you're getting too distracted while you try to work, you have a couple of options.** Either work somewhere (such as the school library) that doesn't have a TV, or break your work down into small chunks – do 20 minutes of maths followed by a quick blast on your favourite game. Just remember to get back to work afterwards!

3 **Do a little bit of work each weekday night.** Although this may be the last thing you feel like doing after being at school all day, if you get it all sorted during the week, it means you won't have any work hanging over you for the whole weekend.

Getting

The Net (or Web if you prefer) can be a wonderful place. It's packed full of every kind of fact you could ever possibly need and it allows you to swap ideas with people on the other side of the world for the price of a local phone call. More than anything, it's very, very big and can be a bit overwhelming if you've never used it before, so here's our guide to making the most of your surf time.

Safe surfing

It's not something you should lie awake worrying about, but sadly there are a very small minority of people out there who use the Internet to help them cause harm to others. If you follow these basic guidelines you should have no problems:

- Have an online nickname, don't use your real name.
- Don't give out any personal details such as phone numbers or addresses.
- Never give out any passwords you might use, such as your hotmail.
- If anyone you meet on the Net makes you feel uncomfortable in any way, tell someone else about it, ideally your parents. Remember, people are not always who they say they are on the Net.

Using the Internet

To get on the Net, you'll obviously need a computer, but the good news is you don't necessarily have to fork out for one yourself. Your school may have an IT club you can join if you want to hone your surfing skills – and if it doesn't then you can always start up a club yourself. Of course, if you've got a computer at home, then even better, just make sure you ask whoever's paying the bills before you embark on an eight-hour multiplayer deathmatch with your mates.

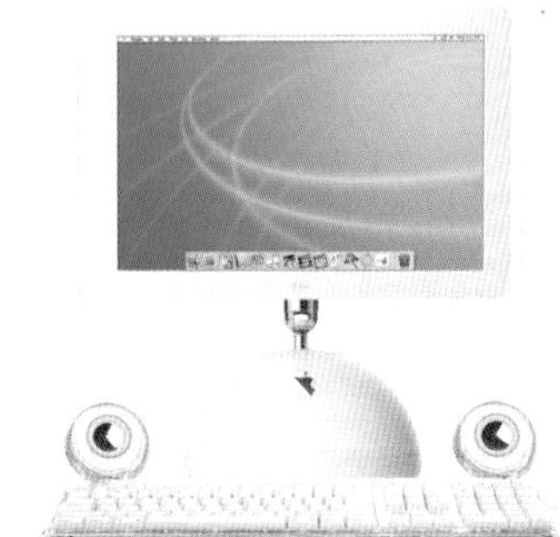

Sites to see www.bbc.co.uk Football and all sorts www.starwars.com Space fans!

On Line

E-mail

One of the first things you'll want to do once you're connected is send an e-mail to all your friends living in such far-flung climes as New York, Sydney, Tokyo, even Wigan. To do this you'll need their e-mail address, which is usually something like their name followed by @ and the name of the company providing their Internet service (eg. harryparker@btinternet.com). Type the address into the 'To' section, add a 'Subject' if you want, then just type your message in the main part of the e-mail. When you're happy, click on the Send & Receive button to 'post' your cyber musings, and next time your pal logs on, the message will be there waiting for him!

Searching the Web

As mentioned before, the Internet is a big old place which can make finding what you are searching for tricky at times, luckily some extremely clever people came up with a special type of Web page designed to make retrieving info that bit easier. Known as search engines, they really couldn't be simpler to use. Type in the address of the search engine (www.google.com and www.yahoo.com are two of the most popular), key in a word or two related to what you're looking for (eg. 'pet rattlesnakes') and click on the 'Search' button. Within seconds, the search engine should come back to you with a whole list of suitable sites. If you're still having problems, try to make your search as broad as possible, for example by using just 'pets' as the keyword.

www.theonering.net For Lord of the Rings buffs   www.wwe.com For wrestling experts!

Puppies, kittens, cute little rabbits with big, floppy ears... you won't find any of them here.

Because this page is all about some of the meanest, most ferocious and most incredibly downright scary animals on the planet.

FIERCE CREATURES

Polar bears

They may look like big, cuddly fellows, but polar bears are the largest land meat-eaters in the world and are known as the only animal that actively hunts down us humans! Don't panic, though – you're unlikely to see one rampaging through your local shopping centre as polar bears are only found on the ice floes of the Arctic.

As well as tucking into the odd human, polar bears also feast on beluga, narwhal, walrus, fish, seabirds, and reindeer. Seals are a particular favourite. Polar bears wait at a breathing hole until a seal approaches, then smash through the snow and ice to snatch the seal with its powerful jaws. They need to be patient, though, as their success rate is just one seal caught every four or five days. Polar bears also have an amazing sense of smell and can detect an animal carcass from 3 km away!

Jaguars

The jaguar is an awesome and scary animal – so much so that the Yanomami Indians have named it the 'Eater of Souls' due to their belief that it feeds on the spirits of the dead! They live mainly in the forest areas of the Americas and, although they look like leopards, they have slightly different markings, a larger and stockier head and body and a shorter tail. They hunt many different types of creature, and kill their prey by piercing the skull with their powerful canine teeth.

Lions

The only cats to live in groups (known as prides), lions mainly hunt by lying in wait and ambushing their prey. The females tend to do most of the hunting, usually working together in groups, while the males defend the pride against intruders, unleashing great roars to warn other lions of possible enemies. There is fierce competition among the males as to who leads the pride, and fights between rivals often end in death for the loser.

Alligators

Alligators are large, deadly reptiles. They float in the water, keeping still, leaving only their eyes and nostrils on view as they wait for their prey. Their huge jaws can easily crush the shell of a passing turtle or the bones of an animal. They've also been known to attack people.

Bull sharks

Great white sharks may have grabbed all the gory glory in films such as 'Jaws' but in fact bull sharks are probably even more deadly than their famous relatives, and may be responsible for many of the attacks on humans that were blamed on great whites. They are unusual in that they spend a lot of time in freshwater, rather than the sea, and have attacked people as far upstream as Baghdad in Iraq. They mainly like to eat other sharks and fish, birds, turtles, dolphins and all manner of crustaceans. As they are found in many different areas of the world, they have a variety of names, such as shovelnose, square-nose and Zambezi shark.

Allsports

Keeping fit, gaining a complete set of new skills, giving you a chance to show off in front of girls... the advantages of taking up a sport are almost endless. It's always good to start off playing a variety of sports so you can find out which one you're best suited to. Once you've made your mind up, you can perhaps specialize more, maybe even joining a club so you can practise to your heart's content. From cycling to curling, there are so many sports that we can't possibly go into them all, so here's a round-up of some of the most popular and exciting.

Tennis

One of the good things about setting your heart on being a tennis ace, is that it's a sport us Brits are known for not being successful at. Our best player, Tim Henman, tries his hardest at Wimbledon every year but even he hasn't won anything of any great note, usually crashing out at the semi-final stage to some Australian or other. So, the scene is set for you to storm in, blasting aces all over the court and grabbing some much-needed glory for your country.

Even though tennis has a reputation of being a sport just for toffs, you don't needs pots of cash to make it to the top. Look, at the Williams sisters – they may be girls, but they could probably give most of the men a run for their money, with just determination, plenty of sponsors and most important of all, pure talent!

WEB LINK: *If you fancy a crack at being the British Lleyton Hewitt, then head along to the Lawn Tennis Association's website for info on your local clubs, at* ***www.lta.org.uk***

Football

Probably the best sport ever invented, and certainly the most popular, there must be literally billions of people across the planet who have dreamed of scoring the winning goal for their country at the World Cup final. Only a tiny few actually get to live out those fantasies, but that shouldn't put you off playing, especially if you're just doing it for fun.

As well as kickabouts with your mates, you could also think about joining the school team, or a local club. Most clubs have a number of teams to suit different age groups and skill levels, so don't worry about feeling out of your depth. If you're serious about the game, then joining a club is also the best way to get spotted by the talent scouts from the professional sides – who knows, before long it could be you stepping out onto that World Cup turf!

WEB LINK: *Look at the 'Grassroots' section at* ***www.thefa.com*** *for information on clubs and leagues in your local area*

Rugby

Rugby is said to have been invented back in 1823 when, during a school game of football, one William Webb Ellis decided to pick the ball up and leg it to the other end of the pitch to 'score'. We're guessing that he probably wasn't the most popular kid at his school, but that hasn't stopped rugby (Union and League) becoming a great sport in its own right. Which position you choose depends on whether you're a slim, pacy type who loves to run with the ball, or if you'd rather get stuck in to some ferocious (but fair) tackles. Join a local or school club and practise, practise, practise. Oh, and, although it's a whole load of fun, be prepared to take some knocks – rugby can be a tough, physical game.

WEB LINK: *Head along to* ***www.rfu.com*** *for all the latest Rugby Union news and discussion.*

Basketball

If you like your sports fast and free-flowing then basketball could be the one for you. And the great thing about it is you don't need any fancy equipment – just a ball and a basket! You also don't have to be seven feet tall to play, as some team positions are more about dribbling and passing the ball than scoring. If your school doesn't have a basketball team, then get in touch with the English Basketball Association (EBBA) and they'll put you in touch with any clubs in your area.

CONTACT: EBBA on telephone 0113 236 1166

CHINESE HOROSCOPES

When they see the word 'horoscopes', most people think about Libra, Gemini, Virgo and all that stuff about 'seeing your future in the stars'. Chinese horoscopes, have a different approach but are just as interesting!

The History Channel

Here's how Chinese horoscopes came about: Basically, the Chinese lunar calendar is 60 years long and is made up of five cycles of 12 years each. Animals were assigned to each of the 60 years. Still with us? Good. Well, according to legend, Buddha summoned all the animals to a big 'do' before he left Earth. Only 12 actually bothered to show up, and these 12 make up the creatures of the Chinese horoscope. Which animal rules the year you were born?

The Rat
(born in 1948, 60, 72, 84, 96)

Rats are busy little fellows, constantly on the go and keen to discover exciting new things. They're workaholics and find it hard to put up their feet and just chill out.

The Tiger
(born in 1950, 62, 74, 86, 98)

Tigers are daredevil types, always trying out new things that no-one else would even dream of doing. Big show-offs!

The Ox
(born in 1949, 61, 73, 85, 97)

Tough, sturdy characters who will stand strong no matter what nastiness life has to throw at them. Oxen are also decent, honest folk who don't suffer fools gladly.

The Rabbit
(born in 1951, 63, 75, 87, 99)

Rabbits are quiet, solitary types who refuse to get stressed out by any hassle or problems. They are, apparently, 'in tune with the pulse of the universe'. Wow, cosmic man.

The Dragon
(born in 1952, 64, 76, 88, 2000)

Despite their sometimes fiery temperament (ho, ho), dragons are energetic creatures and their mere presence is often enough to ward away bad luck. Not the sort of people you'd want to mess with, then.

The Monkey
(born in 1944, 56, 68, 80, 92)

Count yourself very lucky indeed if you're a Monkey. According to the horoscopes, you are both brilliant and extremely imaginative, and can make seemingly impossible tasks look like a total breeze. Cheeky monkeys!

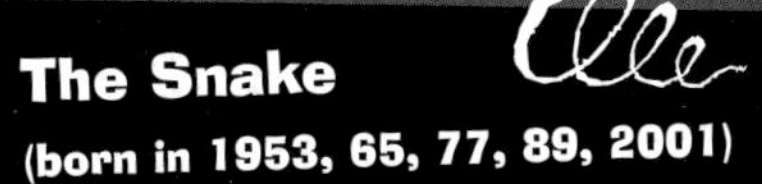

The Snake
(born in 1953, 65, 77, 89, 2001)

Snakes are clever so-and-so's who, once they've started on a project, will stick to it with a quiet, steely determination. All that, and they also 'hold the key to the mysteries of life', according to Chinese legend.

The Rooster
(born in 1945, 57, 69, 81, 93)

Like Snakes, Roosters stick to their assigned tasks with complete dedication. They are also real sticklers for timing, and go into a cold sweat if they're ever late.

The Horse
(born in 1954, 66, 78, 90, 2002)

Horses are so full of energy and life that they can make rats seem like complete layabouts in comparison.

The Dog
(born in 1946, 58, 70, 82, 94)

Dogs are the people to go to if you've got a problem and just want to chat about it as they're always willing to lend an ear (or two).

The Goat
(born in 1955, 67, 79, 91, 2003)

Goats are worth sticking around with as good fortune seems to follow them wherever they go. They're also the sort of people you can tell your secrets to, safe in the knowledge that they won't go around blabbing to others.

The Pig
(born in 1947, 59, 71, 83, 95)

Pigs are caring sorts who get a real kick out of helping other people. They're full of love, innocence and faith. Bless 'em.

Get mixing

Superstar DJs

There used to be a time (ask your parents) when a 'DJ' was either someone who played tunes on the radio, or a lanky, geeky looking bloke carrying a stack of awful records and a large case containing a couple of turntables, some frankly rubbish flashing lights, and bearing the legend 'Mike's Mobile Disco'.

On the Net
Upload your own mixes, or listen to the mixes other people have made at www.skoolhouse.com

Thankfully, all that has changed, and now certain DJs are superstars in their own right, earning cash and achieving levels of fame on a par with actual musicians – just look at Norman 'Fatboy Slim' Cook.

What's your flava?

But if you think that all you have to do is turn up at some swish New York club, stick on a few 'choonz' and leave half an hour later with a fat cheque, then think again. Very few people actually make a living out of being a DJ and building up your reputation will take as much time, hard work and skill as learning to play a musical instrument. You'll also need an almost encyclopedic knowledge of your chosen musical type...

Garage, house,

hip-hop, techno, drum n bass – whether you like your beats fresh, phat or just plain funky, the most important thing is to stay true to yourself and play the music YOU like, not just what you think is popular at the time.

Two turntables and a microphone

Every budding DJ will need the following equipment:

- 2 turntables (with special DJ styli and slipmats)
- 1 mixer
- 1 set of headphones
- 1 playback system (an amp and a pair of speakers)
- and lots of records!

Shop around to find the best deals and ALWAYS try out the gear for yourself – a good shop will have a demo area where you can do just that. Remember, it's you who's going to be using it so you need to be completely sure you're happy before you purchase!

In the mix

A guide to mixing would take up a whole book in its own right so we're just going to give you a few basic tips. Mixing basically means blending two records together so they almost sound like the same track. Creating a smooth, seamless mix is what being a successful DJ is all about, so it helps if you know your records inside out – their beat styles, rhythm patterns, speeds, what sort of beginnings/endings they have and where the breaks are. Then you can match them up with greater ease. As well as listening to the records, take a look at them too – the grooves look different where the beat drops and the breaks come in! From there, you can go on to throw in some samples (taking one part of the next record and playing it in the record you're currently spinning) or, if you're into hip-hop, a bit of scratching. Just experiment until you get something you think sounds good.

August 2003

	school notes/homework	what's on this week
monday 4		
tuesday 5	Neil Armstrong, first man on the Moon, born 1930	
wednesday 6		
thursday 7		
friday 8	Princess Beatrice, 15 today	
saturday 9	An atomic bomb was dropped on Nagasaki, Japan, 1945	
sunday 10	Roy Keane, footballer, 32 today	

FACTS OF THE WEEK

LUCKY CHARMS

Egyptians wore lucky charms called amulets. The charms were meant to protect the wearer from evil spirits and to bring good luck. Children wore amulets shaped like fish to protect them from drowning in the river Nile.

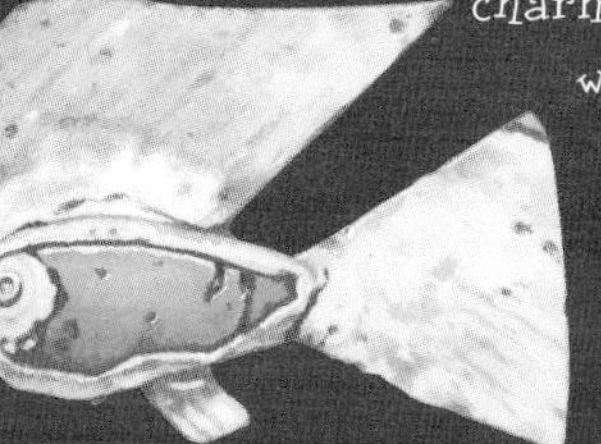

A DAY CAN LAST 21 HOURS!

Night and day happen because Earth is spinning as it circles the Sun. At the height of summer, places near the North Pole are so tilted towards the Sun that it is light almost all day long.

CANTERBURY TALES

In the 1300s an Englishman called Geoffrey Chaucer wrote 'The Canterbury Tales.' These stories were about a group of pilgrims travelling from a London inn to a religious site in Canterbury.

JOKE OF THE WEEK

"What do you get if you cross a tiger with a kangaroo?"
"A stripy jumper!"

QUICK QUIZ

1. Which country does footballer Ronaldo play for?
2. Which brothers flew their aeroplane from Kitty Hawk in 1903?
3. How many lungs does the human body contain?
4. What killed King Harold of England?
5. What do the initials UN stand for?
6. Are whales fish or mammals?

1. Brazil 2. The Wright Brothers 3. Two 4. An arrow 5. United Nations 6. Mammals

ODD ONE OUT

Which of these four countries is the ODD ONE OUT and why?

SPAIN, INDIA, GERMANY, GREECE

India – All the others are European countries

August 2003

	school notes/homework	what's on this week
monday **11**		
tuesday **12**		
wednesday **13**	The last hangings in Britain took place, 1964	
thursday **14**	Japan surrendered to the Allies, 1945	
friday **15**	Napoleon Bonaparte, French emperor, was born 1769	
saturday **16**	Madonna, singer, 45 today	
sunday **17**		

FACTS OF THE WEEK

THE WEATHER FOR LAST WEEK

The earliest weather records are over 3000 years old. They were found on a piece of tortoiseshell and had been written down by Chinese weather watchers. The inscriptions describe when it rained or snowed and how windy it was.

WHEN THE UNITED STATES DOUBLED UP

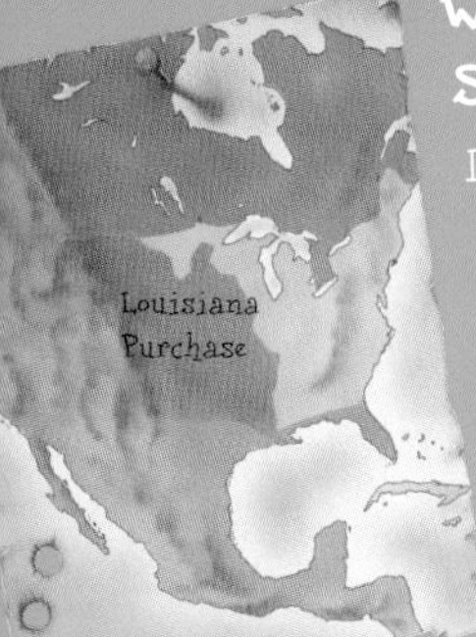

In 1803 the American president, Thomas Jefferson, bought a massive area of land called Louisiana from the French. This was known as the Louisiana Purchase, and included all the land between the Mississippi and the Rocky Mountains.

A STRANGE SIGHT

The Matamata turtle lives only in South America. It is one of the strangest of all turtles, as its head is almost flat, and is shaped like a triangle. It lies on the bottom of rivers and eats fish that swim past.

JOKE OF THE WEEK

"What happened when the lion ate the comedian?"
"He felt funny!"

QUICK QUIZ

1. Where is a rattlesnake's rattle?
2. Which planet is nearest to the Sun?
3. What aid to spelling was first compiled by Dr Samuel Johnson?
4. With which terrorist group is the political party, Sinn Fein, linked?
5. Who was United States president before Bill Clinton?
6. What is 0.5 of 11?

1. In its tail 2. Mercury
3. A dictionary 4. The IRA
5. George Bush 6. 5.5

ODD ONE OUT

Which one of these four is the ODD ONE OUT and why?

BOXER, PERSIAN, SPANIEL, TERRIER

PERSIAN – All the others are breeds of dog

August 2003

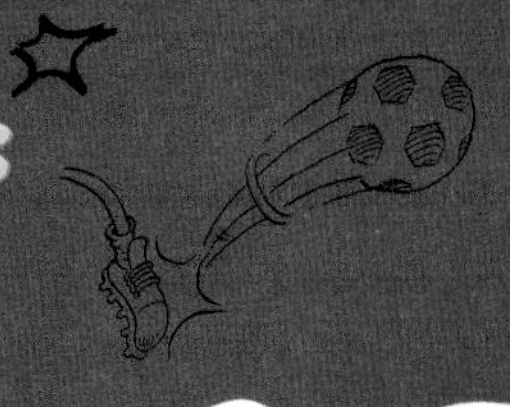

	school notes/homework	what's on this week
monday **18**		
tuesday **19**	Bill Clinton, former US president, 57 today	
wednesday **20**		
thursday **21**	The 'Mona Lisa' painting was stolen from the Louvre in Paris, 1911	
friday **22**	The English Civil War began,1642	
saturday **23**		
sunday **24**	After Vesuvius erupted, Pompeii and Herculaneum were buried under ash, AD79	

FACTS OF THE WEEK

RECORD BREAKERS!

A single boat towed 100 waterskiers! This record was achieved off the coast of Australia in 1986 and no one has beaten it yet. The drag boat was a cruiser called Reef Cat.

KEEP OUT OF ITS WAY!

A tornado is the fastest wind on Earth – it can spin at speeds of 500 kilometres an hour. Tornadoes form over ground that has become very warm. This fast-rising funnel acts as a vacuum cleaner, destroying buildings and lifting cars into the air.

MILLIONS OF YEARS AGO

Dinosaurs lived between 230 million and 65 million years ago. This vast length of time is called the Mesozoic Era. Dinosaurs were around for about 80 times longer than people have been on Earth!

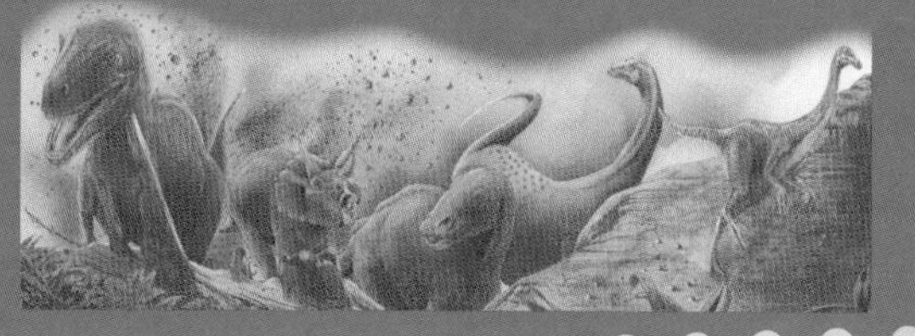

JOKE OF THE WEEK

"What's striped and bouncy?"
"A tiger on a pogo stick!"

QUICK QUIZ

1. What nationality is bowler Darren Gough?
2. What does Michael Fish do on television?
3. Which English general gave his name to a type of rubber boot?
4. What currency do Canadians use?
5. How many days are in the month of April?
6. Which creature finally eats Captain Hook?

1. English 2. He's a weatherman 3. Duke of Wellington 4. Canadian dollars 5. 30 6. A crocodile

WORD SEARCH

Try and find five English counties hidden in the word search below:

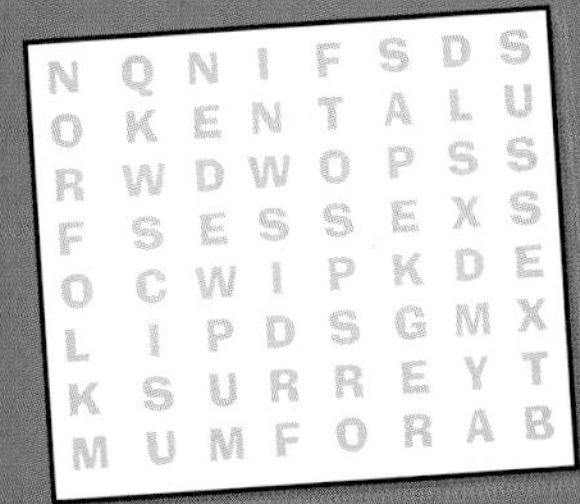

August 2003

	school notes/homework	what's on this week
monday **25**	Sean Connery, actor ,73 today	
tuesday **26**	Julius Caesar landed in Britain, 55BC	
wednesday **27**		
thursday **28**		
friday **29**	Michael Jackson, singer, 45 today	
saturday **30**	Cameron Diaz, actress, 31 today	
sunday **31**	Henry VI ascended the English throne aged 9 months, 1422	

FACTS OF THE WEEK

KEEP AN EYE OUT

A meteor shower is a dramatic display of shooting stars. For a short period more than a thousand a second may flash across the sky. August is the best month to see one.

NEW SHOES

Booby birds dance to attract a mate. There are two types of booby, blue-or red-footed. The dancing draws attention to the male's colourful feet. Perhaps this stops the females from mating with the wrong type of bird.

WHAT A DOG!

A dog named Laika was the first living thing to go into space. In 1957 she travelled in a Russian spacecraft called 'Sputnik 2', and stayed in space for two weeks.

JOKE OF THE WEEK

"What do you get if you cross an elephant with a kangaroo?"
"Big holes all over Australia!"

QUICK QUIZ

1. Was the dinosaur Brontosaurus a meat or plant eater?
2. What happens to a deciduous tree in Autumn?
3. On what continent are penguins found?
4. How long does an unborn human baby spend inside its mother?
5. What was the name of the sword in the tales of King Arthur?
6. How did Joan of Arc die?

1. Plant eater 2. Its leaves fall off 3. Antarctica
4. Nine months 5. Excalibur
6. She was burned at the stake

ODD ONE OUT

Can you spot the odd band out?

TAKE THAT, WESTLIFE, ATOMIC KITTEN, BLUE

Atomic Kitten – All the others are boys only

September 2003

	school notes/homework	what's on this week
monday 1	Poland was invaded by Germany, 1939	
tuesday 2	Lennox Lewis, boxer, 38 today	
wednesday 3	Britain and France declared war on Germany, 1939	
thursday 4		
friday 5		
saturday 6	Greg Rusedski, tennis player, 30 today	
sunday 7	Elizabeth I, Queen of England, was born 1533	

FACTS OF THE WEEK

MAKING MUSIC

Most crickets chirp by rubbing together their wings. The bases of the wings near the body have hard, ridged strips like rows of pegs. These click past each other to make the chirping sound.

UNDERSEA GOD

Neptune (or Poseidon) was an undersea god. Poseidon was the name used by the ancient Greeks and Neptune by the ancient Romans. Both civilizations pictured their god with a fork called a trident. They blamed their gods for the terrible storms that wrecked boats in the Mediterranean.

EUREKA!

A scientist called Archimedes lived in Greece over 2000 years ago. He made some important discoveries in physics and mathematics. He made one discovery while in the bath and ran into the street without any clothes, shouting "Eureka!" which means 'I have found it'.

JOKE OF THE WEEK

"What looks like half a cat?"
"The other half!"

QUICK QUIZ

1. Used in World War II, what sort of device were U-boats?
2. Who led the Gunpowder Plot?
3. What letter is usually followed by u in English words?
4. What part of your body features a pupil and a cornea?
5. What is a half plus an eighth?
6. Who is Batman's sidekick?

1. Submarines 2. Guy Fawkes
3. Q 4. The eye
5. Five-eighths 6. Robin

NAME SCRAMBLE

A former member of a girl band and wife to a famous footballer, is hidden in these letters. Who is it?

ITVCIOAR CHMAKBE

VICTORIA BECKHAM

September 2003

	school notes/homework	what's on this week
monday 8	Italy surrendered to the Allies, 1943	
tuesday 9		
wednesday 10		
thursday 11	The Scots, led by William Wallace, defeated the English at Stirling Bridge, 1297	
friday 12		
saturday 13	New York became the capital of the United States, 1788	
sunday 14		

FACTS OF THE WEEK

FLOWING SEAS

There are streams in the oceans. All the water in the oceans is constantly moving, but in some places it flows as currents, which take particular paths. One of these is the warm Gulf Stream, that travels around the edge of the Atlantic Ocean.

LOVING TO DEATH!

Courtship is a dangerous time for the hunting insect called the praying mantis. The female is much bigger than the male, and as soon as they have mated, she may eat him!

RECORD BREAKING ROBOT

Jurassic Park's nine species of dinosaurs thundered and roared through the world's cinemas in 1993. Made of latex and foam rubber, the dinosaur robots were incredibly realistic. They included the largest film robot ever made a – 5.5-m tall Tyrannosaurus rex.

JOKE OF THE WEEK

"What happened when the cat ate a ball of wool?"
"She had mittens!"

QUICK QUIZ

1. How many days are there in seven weeks?
2. Which planet is the largest in our Solar System?
3. Which is the world's biggest shark: the whale shark, the great white shark or the tiger shark?
4. What was the name of the girl who met the Mad Hatter and the Queen of Hearts?
5. What caused the Titanic to sink in 1912?
6. What is 'Sporty Spice', Mel C's real name?

1. 49 2. Jupite
3. The whale shark 4. Alice
5. Hitting an iceberg
6. Melanie Chisholm

WORD SEARCH

Find the five BIRDS OF PREY hiding in this word search

E	A	G	L	E	E	W	Q
V	U	L	T	U	R	E	W
U	B	U	Z	Z	A	R	D
L	E	A	R	O	D	O	E
T	F	A	L	C	O	N	P
N	B	S	O	W	L	C	D
P	M	C	E	W	T	Y	U
A	J	K	I	S	F	A	B

September 2003

	school notes/homework	what's on this week
monday 15	Prince Harry, 19 today	
tuesday 16		
wednesday 17	Des Lynam, broadcaster, 61 today	
thursday 18		
friday 19	The first Mickey Mouse cartoon, 'Steamboat Willie', was shown, 1928	
saturday 20		
sunday 21	Liam Gallagher, singer, 31 today	

FACTS OF THE WEEK

WATERSPORT

Jetskiers can travel at nearly 100 kilometres per hour. Jetskis were developed in the 1960s. Their inventor was an American called Clayton Jacobsen who wanted to combine his two favourite hobbies – motorbikes and waterskiing.

WELL TRAINED

It took about 14 years of training to become a knight. The son of a noble joined a lord's household aged seven. After training he became a squire, and he learned how to fight with a sword. If successful, he became a knight at 21.

FIGHTING FOR HUMAN RIGHTS

Nelson Mandela was the first black president of South Africa (1994–99). As a young man he fought for the rights of black South Africans. White leaders imprisoned him for his beliefs for 28 years (1962–90).

JOKE OF THE WEEK

"What do you get if you cross a cat with a parrot?"
"A carrot!"

QUICK QUIZ

1. Who is the world number one in golf?
2. Which king was known as 'The Lionheart'?
3. Which two countries does Hadrian's Wall separate?
4. What are the three emergency services?
5. What disaster hit London in 1666?
6. What subject has Delia Smith written many successful books about?

1. Tiger Woods 2. Richard I
3. England and Scotland
4. Police Fire and Ambulance
5. The Great Fire 6. Cookery

WORD SCRAMBLE

Unscramble the letters to find three famous cities:

DADIRM, HTANES, EOMR

MADRID, ATHENS, ROME

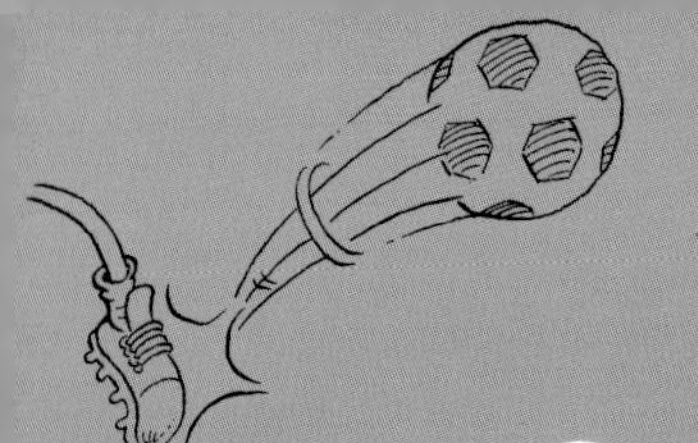

September 2003

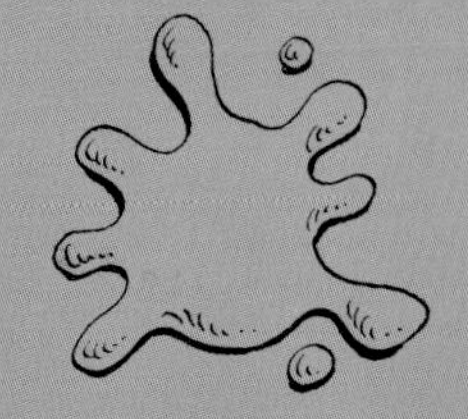

	school notes/homework	what's on this week
monday **22**		
tuesday **23**	Johann Gottfried Galle discovered the planet Neptune, 1846	
wednesday **24**		
thursday **25**	Will Smith, actor and singer, 35 today	
friday **26**		
saturday **27**	Serina Williams, tennis player, 22 today	
sunday **28**	'God Save the King' sung for the first time, Drury Lane, 1745	

FACTS OF THE WEEK

LOVE DANCE

Some insects flash bright lights as they fly. The firefly is not a fly but a type of beetle. In a courtship display the male fireflies 'dance' in the air at dusk, the rear parts of their bodies glowing on and off about once each second.

SINKING SUCCESS

'Titanic' (1997) is the only film since 'Ben-Hur' (1959) to have won 11 oscars. More than 100 stunt artists helped to recreate the sinking scene. The stunt team spent a record 6000 hours on the set of 'Titanic' – the equivalent of almost 17 years for one person!

WHAT'S YOUR NAME?

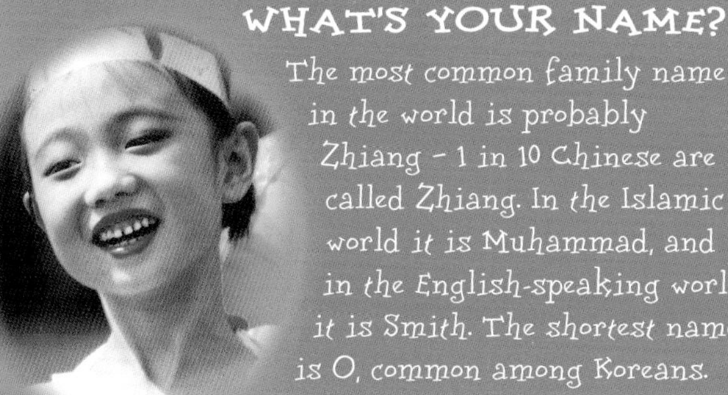

The most common family name in the world is probably Zhiang – 1 in 10 Chinese are called Zhiang. In the Islamic world it is Muhammad, and in the English-speaking world it is Smith. The shortest name is O, common among Koreans.

JOKE OF THE WEEK

"What sleeps at the bottom of the sea?"
"A kipper!"

QUICK QUIZ

1. What mammal makes large dams out of wood?
2. How many threes are in 39?
3. Complete the title of the Shakespeare play, 'The Taming of...'?
4. Who was the famous gangster responsible for the St Valentine's Day Massacre?
5. What body part are biceps and triceps?
6. Which wife of King Henry VIII is said to have had six fingers on one hand?

1. The beaver 2. 13
3. The Taming of the Shrew
4. Al Capone 5. Muscles
6. Anne Boleyn

NAME SCRAMBLE

Which famous footballer is hidden in these letters?

DONALRO

RONALDO

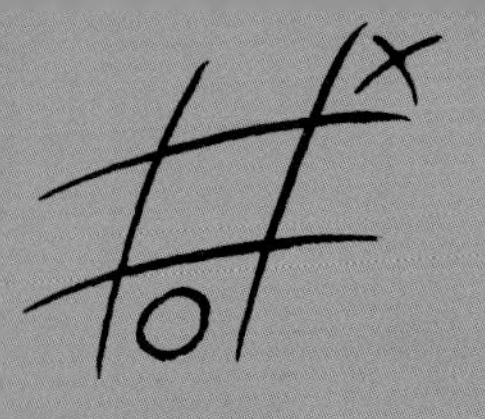

September/October 2003

	school notes/homework	what's on this week
monday **29**		
tuesday **30**	Martina Hingis, tennis player, 23 today	
wednesday **1**	Walt Disney World opened in Orlando, Florida, 1971	
thursday **2**	Sting (Gordon Sumner), singer, 52 today	
friday **3**		
saturday **4**	The first public escalator opened at Earl's Court, London, 1911	
sunday **5**		

FACTS OF THE WEEK

CAMELOT

King Arthur had many castle homes but his favourite was Camelot. Historians think that Camelot was really an English castle called Tintagel. The remains of this castle can still be explored in the county of Cornwall.

SOME WERE REALLY CUTE!

The name 'dinosaur' means 'terrible lizard'. But dinosaurs weren't lizards, and not all dinosaurs were terrible. Small plant-eating dinosaurs were about as 'terrible' as today's sheep!

WHAT LIES BENEATH

Long ago, people believed in a giant sea monster, called the kraken. The stories were used to explain the dangers of the sea. Sightings of the giant squid with eyes as big as dinner plates, might have inspired these tales.

JOKE OF THE WEEK

"What do you call an elephant that flies?"
"A jumbo jet!"

QUICK QUIZ

1. How many dalmations were there in the famous Disney film?
2. What weight does Lennox Lewis box at?
3. Who married Prince Edward in 1999?
4. Where is Mount Snowdon?
5. In cockney rhyming slang, what does 'apples and pears' mean?
6. What are the five vowels?

1. 101 2. Heavyweight
3. Sophie Rhys-Jones
4. Wales 5. Stairs
6. A E I O U

LETTER PUZZLE

Where would you see these letters shown in this order?

ZXCVBNM

On a typewriter or computer keyboard

October 2003

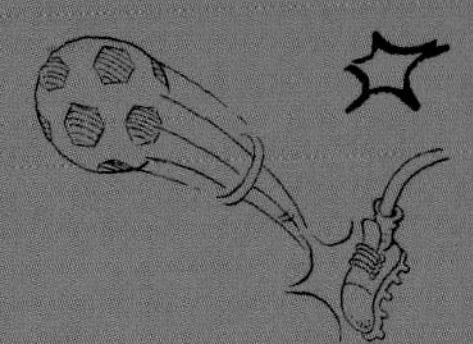

	school notes/homework	what's on this week
monday 6	'The Jazz Singer', first full-length talking film, shown, 1927	
tuesday 7		
wednesday 8		
thursday 9	John Lennon, singer-songwriter, was born 1940	
friday 10		
saturday 11	Dawn French, comedian, 46 today	
sunday 12	Luciano Pavarotti, opera singer, 68 today	

FACTS OF THE WEEK

CHANGE OF HORSE

A rich medieval knight would have three horses. He rode his heaviest horse for fighting and tournaments. He also had a horse for riding, and a baggage horse. The best horses were warhorses from Italy and Spain. They were quick, strong and sturdy.

TRICK OF THE LIGHT

Oceans can look blue, green or grey. This is because of the way light hits the surface. Water soaks up the red parts of light but scatters the blue-green parts, making the sea look different shades of blue or green.

STICKY FEET

The gecko is a lizard found in most warm countries. The tree gecko has hairs on its feet, which have a sticking effect. This enables it to walk on any surface, and even hang on by just one toe!

JOKE OF THE WEEK

"What do you get if you cross a tiger with a snowman?"
"Frostbite!"

QUICK QUIZ

1. Who did Fagin and the Artful Dodger take under their wing?
2. How many years can a lion live to: 12, 20 or 30?
3. Where would you find your femur bone?
4. What is a monsoon?
5. With what films do you associate Darth Maul and Darth Vader?
6. What country was once ruled by shoguns?

1. Oliver Twist 2. 30
3. In your leg 4. A wind which brings heavy rains
5. Star Wars 6. Japan

ODD ONE OUT

Which of these four is the ODD ONE OUT and why?

REMBRANT, CONSTABLE, MONET, SHAKESPEARE

SHAKESPEARE – All the others are artists

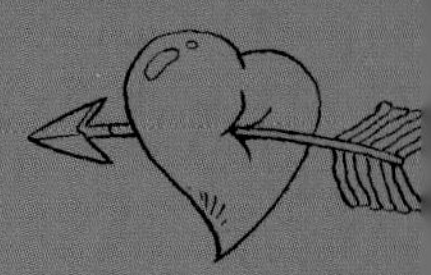

October 2003

	school notes/homework	what's on this week
monday 13	Margaret Thatcher, former prime minister, 78 today	
tuesday 14	The Battle of Hastings was fought, 1066	
wednesday 15	The Duchess of York, 44 today	
thursday 16		
friday 17	Marshall Mathers (Eminem), rapper, 29 today	
saturday 18		
sunday 19		

FACTS OF THE WEEK

AM I AN INSECT?

A spider has eight legs. So it's not an insect! It's a type of animal called an arachnid. All spiders are deadly hunters. They have large fanglike jaws which they use to grab and stab their prey. The fangs inject a poison to kill or quieten the victim before being eaten.

WORST EVER HURRICANE IN BRITAIN

Britain's worst storm of modern times was the hurricane of October, 1987. High winds uprooted and blew down 15 million trees in southern England, blocked roads, and brought down roofs and power lines.

DANGEROUS WORK

Marie Curie and her husband Pierre were scientists who worked in France in the late 1800s and early 1900s. Marie Curie was a clever and hard-working physicist who discovered a dangerous but useful chemical substance called radium.

JOKE OF THE WEEK

"What lights up a football stadium?"
"A football match!"

QUICK QUIZ

1. Who was alleged to have said 'We are not amused'?
2. What country does Ryan Giggs play for?
3. What was the painter Van Gogh's first name?
4. What does the French word 'Bonjour' mean?
5. What was unusual about the childhood of the twins who founded Rome?
6. Who had a teddy bear nicknamed Winnie the Pooh?

1. Queen Victoria 2. Wales 3. Vincent 4. Hello or good day 5. They were brought up by wolves 6. Christopher Robin

BIRD SEARCH

Try and find the five garden birds hidden in the word search below.

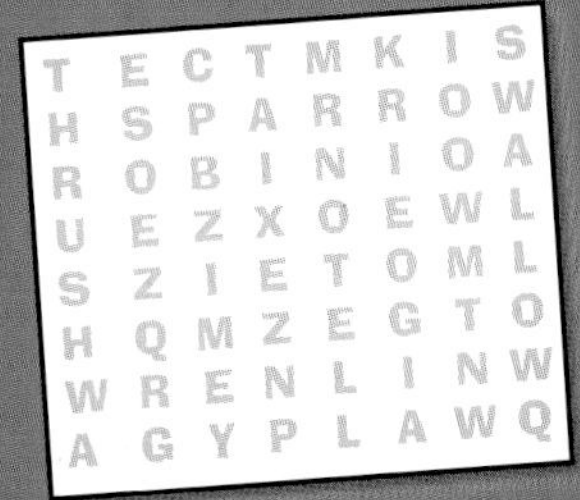

October 2003

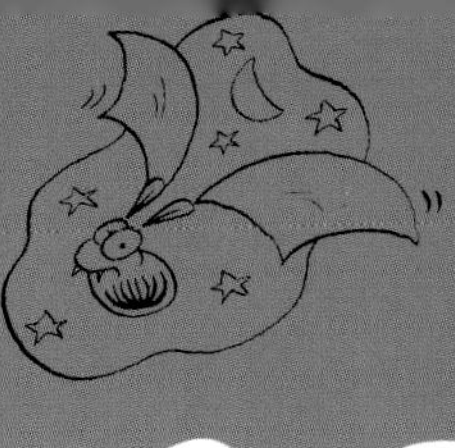

	school notes/homework	what's on this week
monday 20		
tuesday 21	Horatio Nelson killed at the Battle of Trafalgar, 1805	
wednesday 22		
thursday 23	Pelé, Brazilian footballer, 63 today	
friday 24		
saturday 25	The English defeated the French at the Battle of Agincourt, 1415	
sunday 26	The English Football Association formed, 1863	

FACTS OF THE WEEK

NATURAL CREATIONS

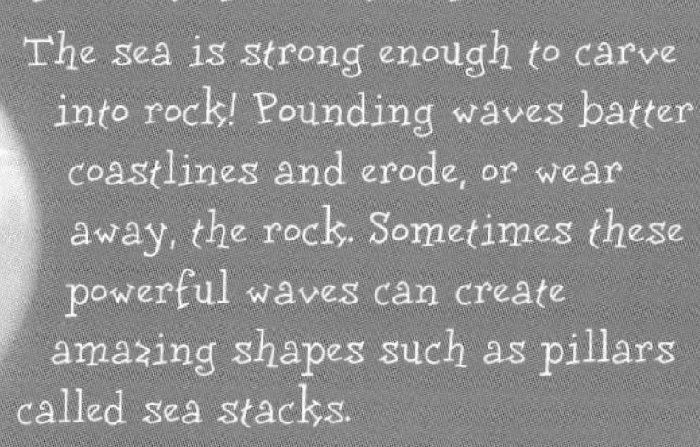

The sea is strong enough to carve into rock! Pounding waves batter coastlines and erode, or wear away, the rock. Sometimes these powerful waves can create amazing shapes such as pillars called sea stacks.

PUNK CULTURE

Punk was a fad of 1970s youth culture and it started a craze for body art that is still popular. Ripped clothes, safety-pin piercings, chains, studs and spiky coloured hair were worn as an expression of freedom and a rebellion against conformity.

SHIPS IN THE SKY

The world's biggest airships were the Hindenberg, destroyed by fire in 1937, and the Graf Zeppelin II, last used in 1940. They were 245 metres long and carried 75 passengers plus 25 crew, gliding almost silently above the oceans.

JOKE OF THE WEEK

"What are baby lobsters called?"
"Nippers!"

QUICK QUIZ

1. Where is Britain's one tennis grand slam tournament played?
2. Which movie actor has the nickname 'Sly'?
3. What is the capital of Spain?
4. Would you fish with, eat or kick a melon ball?
5. What type of event was Woodstock?
6. In which decade did Woodstock occur?

1. Wimbledon 2. Sylvester Stallone 3. Madrid 4. Eat it 5. A music festival 6. The 1960s

ODD SONG OUT

Which song is the odd one out and why?

YESTERDAY, HELP, MY GIRL, LET IT BE

MY GIRL – All the others are by the Beatles

October/November 2003

	school notes/homework	what's on this week
monday 27		
tuesday 28	Julia Roberts, actress, 36 today	
wednesday 29	Sir Walter Raleigh, was executed, 1618	
thursday 30	Benito Mussolini seized power in Italy, 1922	
friday 31	The Battle of Britain ended, 1940	
saturday 1	Lisbon, capital of Portugal, was destroyed by an earthquake, 1755	
sunday 2	'The Sunday Express' carried the first crossword puzzle in a British newspaper, 1924	

FACTS OF THE WEEK

INSECT LEAPER

The click beetle is about 12 millimetres long. When in danger it falls on its back and pretends to be dead. But it slowly arches its body and then straightens with a jerk and a 'click'. It can flick itself about 25 centimetres into the air!

FRIGHTENINGLY FUNNY

Over the centuries, many sinister figures from traditional myths and legends have been turned into pleasant or harmless characters. For example, the movie Hocus Pocus features three silly, clumsy witches outwitted by a group of children.

PREDICTING THE FUTURE

Roman people were very superstitious. They believed that they could foretell the future by observing animals, birds, insects and even the weather! For example, bees were a sign of riches and happiness but a hooting owl foretold danger.

JOKE OF THE WEEK

"What is the most slippery country in the world?"

"Greece!"

QUICK QUIZ

1. What were the Zero, the Me109 and the Spitfire?
2. What do you do if you 'chance your arm'?
3. Is a prickly pear: a type of tree, cactus or wallflower?
4. How many sides has a pentagon?
5. How many holes are on a standard golf course?
6. For which sport did Michael Jordan become famous?

1. World War II fighter aircraft
2. Take a risk 3. A cactus
4. Five 5. 18 6. Basketball

HALLOWEEN SEARCH

Hidden below are five halloween words for you to find!

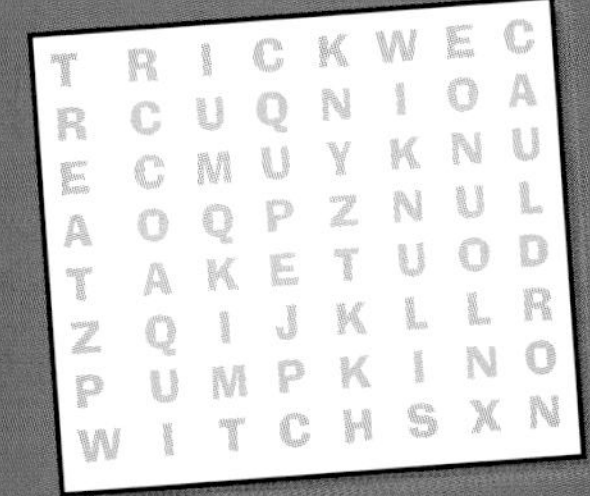

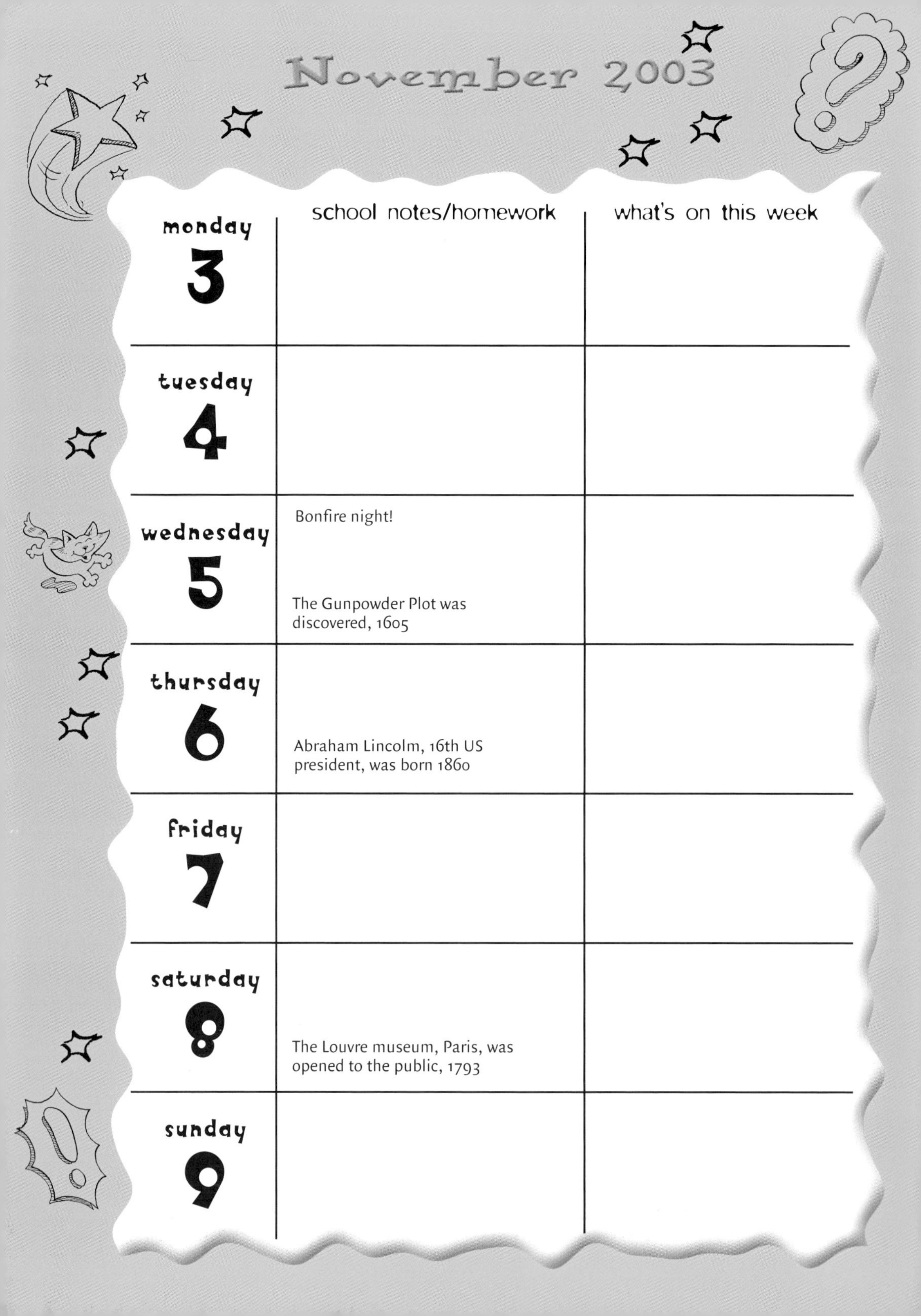

November 2003

	school notes/homework	what's on this week
monday 3		
tuesday 4		
wednesday 5	Bonfire night! The Gunpowder Plot was discovered, 1605	
thursday 6	Abraham Lincolm, 16th US president, was born 1860	
friday 7		
saturday 8	The Louvre museum, Paris, was opened to the public, 1793	
sunday 9		

FACTS OF THE WEEK

FROM NORTH TO SOUTH

The spinning Earth acts like a magnet. At the centre of the Earth is liquid iron. As the Earth spins, it makes the iron behave like a magnet with a North and South Pole. These act on the magnet in a compass to make the needle point to the North and South Poles.

MACBETH

Glamis Castle in Scotland is the scene for the play 'Macbeth' by William Shakespeare. In the play, the ambitious Macbeth plots with his evil wife to kill the Scottish king, Duncan, and claim the throne for himself. In real life, Macbeth did defeat and kill Duncan in 1040.

CREATURES EVEN OLDER THAN DINOSAURS!

Dinosaurs were not the first animals on Earth. Many other kinds of creatures lived before them, including many other types of reptiles. Over millions of years one of these groups of reptiles probably changed very slowly, or evolved, into the first dinosaurs.

JOKE OF THE WEEK

"What might you eat in Paris?"
"The trifle tower!"

QUICK QUIZ

1. With which instrument is Jimi Hendrix associated?
2. In which ocean are the islands of Hawaii situated?
3. How many ten pence pieces are there in £20?
4. What does the Roman numeral V equal?
5. What type of shop first opened in Britain in 1948?
6. How many people speak in a monologue?

1. Electric guitar
2. The Pacific 3. 200
4. Five 5. A supermarket
6. One

WORD SCRAMBLE

Try and guess the BONFIRE NIGHT word in the scramble below!

RESGNAB!

BANGERS!

November 2003

	school notes/homework	what's on this week
monday **10**		
tuesday **11**	World War I ended, 1918	
wednesday **12**		
thursday **13**		
friday **14**	Prince Charles, 55 today	
saturday **15**		
sunday **16**	Paul Scholes, footballer, 29 today	

FACTS OF THE WEEK

SETTING A TRAP

The trapdoor spider lives in a burrow with a wedge-shaped door made from silk. The spider hides just behind this door. When it detects a small animal passing, it opens the door and rushes out to grab its victim.

HE WHO MUST BE OBEYED

A Roman father had the power of life and death over his family. According to Roman law, each family had to be headed by a man. He was known as the 'paterfamilias' (father of a family), and was usually the oldest surviving male.

THE FASTEST SUPERSONIC AIRLINER

Only 16 Concordes were ever built, as a joint project between Britain and France. The world's only commercial supersonic airliner flew at 2,300 km/h, crossing the Atlantic in under three hours. No Concorde had ever crashed until 2000.

QUICK QUIZ

1. Which Charles wrote 'Great Expectations'?
2. What are the names of the two types of elephant?
3. What planet did the two Viking spacecraft land on?
4. What are Monza and Brands Hatch?
5. Which composer wrote The Four Seasons?
6. If you were at King's Cross railway station in London, would you be getting on a train that heads north, south or east?

1. Charles Dickens
2. Indian and African 3. Mars
4. Motor racing tracks
5. Vivaldi 6. North

JOKE OF THE WEEK

"What has two humps and is found at the North Pole?"
"A lost camel!"

WORD PUZZLE

Which similar sounding words mean the following?

(a) FIERCE FURRY ANIMAL/NO CLOTHES ON (b) A NEAT PATTERN/AS GOOD AS MONEY

(a) bear/bare (b) check/cheque

November 2003
school notes/homework
what's on this week
monday 17
tuesday 18
William Tell shot an apple off his son's head, 1307
wednesday 19
thursday 20
friday 21
saturday 22
President Kennedy was assassinated in Dallas, 1963
sunday 23

FACTS OF THE WEEK

KING ARTHUR AND EXCALIBUR

Legend says that King Arthur became king after pulling a magic sword called Excalibur out of a stone. This act proved that he was the right person to rule Britain. People have written stories about Arthur and the Knights of the Round Table, for more than 1000 years.

NATURAL RESOURCE

In Iceland, underground steam is used to make lights work. The steam is sent to power stations and is used to work generators to make electricity. The electricity then flows to homes and powers electrical equipment such as lights, televisions and computers.

ITS JUST AND ILLUSION

Flying fish cannot really fly. Fish can't survive out of water, but flying fish sometimes leap above the waves when they are travelling at high speeds. They use their winglike fins to keep them in the air for as long as 30 seconds.

JOKE OF THE WEEK

"Why aren't football stadiums built in outer space?"
"Because there is no atmosphere!"

QUICK QUIZ

1. Which Scottish city is famous for its summer festival of the arts?
2. Where would you find woofers and tweeters?
3. How many different Catherines did King Henry VIII marry?
4. What sort of stories are associated with the writer Hans Christian Andersen?
5. Are mammals warm- or cold-blooded?
6. What is 50% of 122?

1. Edinburgh 2. Loudspeakers
3. Three 4. Fairy tales
5. Warm-blooded 6. 61

NAME SCRAMBLE

Which popular holiday destination is hidden in these letters?

ZABII

IBIZA

November 2003

	school notes/homework	what's on this week
monday **24**	Billy Connolly, comedian, 61 today	
tuesday **25**		
wednesday **26**		
thursday **27**	Alred Nobel establishes the Nobel Prize, 1895	
friday **28**		
saturday **29**	St. Andrew's Day Ryan Giggs, footballer, 30 today	
sunday **30**	Sir Winston Churchill, former prime minister, was born 1874	

FACTS OF THE WEEK

NO PADDLING TODAY

Tidal waves are the most powerful waves. Also known as tsunamis, they happen when underwater earthquakes trigger tremendous shock waves. These whip up a wall of water that travels across the sea's surface.

SOUND SYSTEMS

Mole-crickets get their name from the way they tunnel through soil, like real moles. The burrow entrance is specially shaped, almost like the loudspeaker of a music system. It makes the crickets chirps sound louder and travel farther.

THE CHAMPIONS!

The ultimate football prize, the World Cup Trophy is presented to the winning team every four years. Countries qualify for the final stages through an elimination series. Brazil are the only nation to have played in every World Cup finals stage.

JOKE OF THE WEEK

"What's the chilliest ground in the premiership?"
"Cold Trafford!"

QUICK QUIZ

1. Which TV show features the characters Dot Cotton and Phil Mitchell?
2. What type of creature was the star of 'Jaws'?
3. Which saint is Santa Claus named after?
4. What is called London's third airport?
5. Do all insects lay eggs?
6. How many sides has a hexagon?

1. EastEnders 2. A shark
3. St Nicholas 4. Stansted
5. Yes 6. Six

ODD ONE OUT

Which musical instrument is the odd one out and why?

OBOE, VIOLIN, FLUTE, RECORDER

VIOLIN – All the others are wind instruments

December 2003

	school notes/homework	what's on this week
monday 1		
tuesday 2	Britney Spears, singer, 22 today	
wednesday 3		
thursday 4		
friday 5	Walt Disney, creator of 'Mickey Mouse', was born 1901	
saturday 6	Thomas Edison makes the 1st sound recording, 1877	
sunday 7		

FACTS OF THE WEEK

LOOKING OUT FOR FOSSILS

Some fossils look like coiled snakes but are really shellfish called ammonites. An ammonite's body was covered by a spiral shell. The body rotted away leaving the shell to become the fossil. Ammonites lived in the seas at the same time as the dinosaurs lived on land.

WELL BEHAVED

Medieval knights had to behave according to a set of rules, known as the 'code of chivalry'. The code involved being brave and honourable on the battlefield, and treating the enemy politely and fairly. It also instructed knights how to behave towards women.

SQUATTERS' RIGHTS

Most crabs shed their shells as they outgrow them, but the hermit crab does not have a shell. It borrows the leftover shell of a dead whelk or other mollusc – whatever it can squeeze into to protect its soft body.

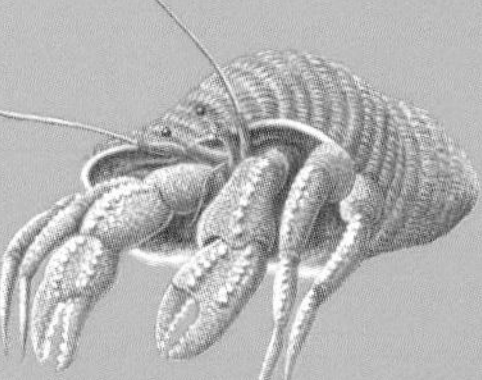

JOKE OF THE WEEK

"How did the footbal pitch end up as triangle?"
"Somebody took a corner!"

QUICK QUIZ

1. Which Sheriff was an enemy of Robin Hood?
2. Was the Battle of Agincourt a land or sea battle?
3. What does the abbreviation HMS stand for?
4. What type of bird would you find in a gaggle?
5. How many sides does a triangle have?
6. What letter can be added to hat to mean talk?

1. Sheriff of Nottingham
2. A land battle 3. His, or Her Majesty's Ship 4.Geese
5. Three 6. (C) Chat

WORD SEARCH

Can you find the names of five British cities below?

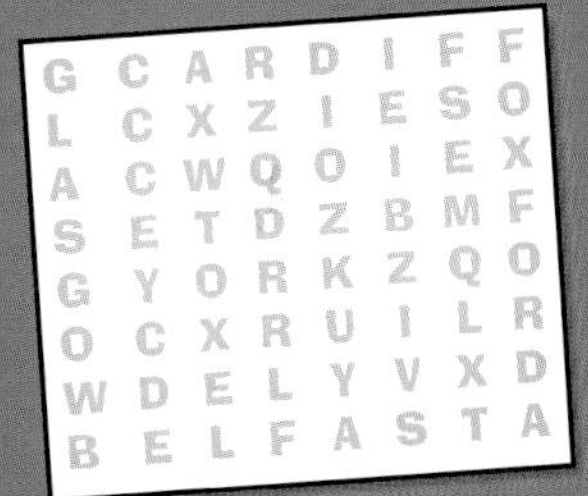

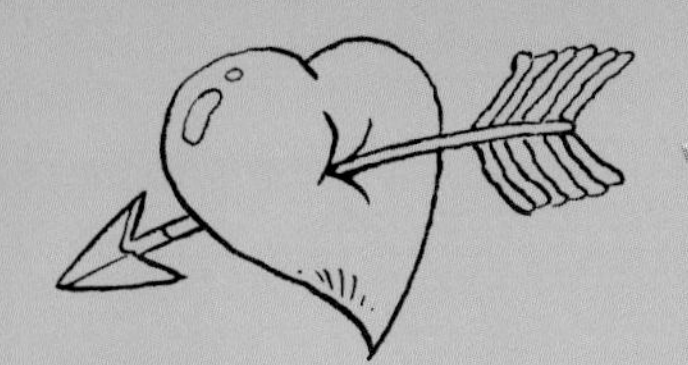

December 2003

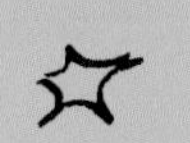

	school notes/homework	what's on this week
monday **8**	The first traffic lights were erected in London, 1868	
tuesday **9**		
wednesday **10**	The first episode of 'Coronation Street' was televised, 1960	
thursday **11**	The first motor show opened in Paris, 1894	
friday **12**		
saturday **13**		
sunday **14**	Michael Owen, footballer, 24 today	

FACTS OF THE WEEK

OUT OF ACTION

This gold leaf crab spider has caught a honeybee. Its venom works fast to paralyse the bee. If it did not, the bee's struggling might harm the spider and draw the attention of the spider's enemies.

ANIMAL LOVERS

Roman families liked to keep pets. Roman statues and paintings show many children playing with their pets. Dogs, cats and doves were all popular. Some families also kept ornamental fish and tame deer.

DEAD AS A DODO

The dodo lived undisturbed on the island of Mauritius in the Indian Ocean until European sailors arrived in the 1500s. Sailors killed the birds for food, and rats and cats ate the eggs. By 1680 the dodo was extinct.

JOKE OF THE WEEK

"Which goalkeeper can jump higher than a crossbar?"
"All of them, a crossbar can't jump!"

QUICK QUIZ

1. Which religious leader lives in the Vatican City?
2. Which country's flag is a red circle on a white background?
3. If you were born on March 7, what would your star sign be?
4. How many strings does a violin have?
5. In 1980 which former actor became President of the United States?
6. Which town is closely associated with Shakespeare?

1. The Pope 2. Japan
3. Pisces 4. Four
5. Ronald Reagan
6. Stratford-upon-Avon

NAME THE GROUPS

What are groups of the following animals called?

(a) WOLVES (b) GEESE
(c) BEES (d) CROWS
(e) ELEPHANTS

(a) pack (b) gaggle (c) swarm
(d) murder (e) herd

December 2003

	school notes/homework	what's on this week
monday 15		
tuesday 16	Ludwig van Beethoven, composer, was born 1770	
wednesday 17	The Wright Brothers made their first flight at Kitty Hawk, North Carolina, 1903	
thursday 18	Brad Pitt, actor, 40 today	
friday 19		
saturday 20		
sunday 21	Shortest Day 'Snow White and the Seven Dwarfs', first full-length colour cartoon, shown, 1937	

FACTS OF THE WEEK

WHAT A WEAPON!

Hammerhead sharks have a hammer-shaped head! With a nostril and an eye on each end of the 'hammer', they swing their head from side to side. This gives them double the chance to see and sniff out any signs of a tasty catch.

REGGAE MUSIC

Reggae is a type of dance music from Jamaica, noted for its use of a heavy offbeat rhythm. It was made world-famous in the 1970s by Bob Marley (1945-81) and his group The Wailers. He had a string of hits before his early death at the age of 34.

FOR A CUP OF TEA

Drinking tea is a strong cultural tradition in many parts of the world - notably Japan, China, India and Britain. In much of Asia, the people who grow and pick the tea are poor workers, while those who enjoy it are rich consumers.

JOKE OF THE WEEK

"Why did a footballer take a piece of rope onto the pitch?"

"He was the skipper!"

QUICK QUIZ

1. How many brothers does Princess Anne have?
2. Name one of the two packs of cards in the middle of a Monopoly board?
3. What nationality was the painter Claude Monet?
4. What was so amazing about the pig called Babe?
5. How many people attended Mozart's funeral: 1, 40, 100 or 1000?
6. Which is the higher belt in Judo: black or yellow?

1. Three 2. Chance and Community Chest
3. French 4. It could talk
5. One 6. Black

NAME THE NATIVE

What are the people who live in the following countries called?

(a) SWITZERLAND
(b) MALTA
(c) HOLLAND (d) EGYPT

(a) Swiss (b) Maltese (c) Dutch
(d) Egyptian

December 2003

	school notes/homework	what's on this week
monday 22		
tuesday 23	Ireland is divided into 2 parts, each with it's own parliament, 1920	
wednesday 24	Christmas Eve	
thursday 25	Christmas Day Sir Isaac Newton, scientist, was born 1642	
friday 26	Boxing Day	
saturday 27		
sunday 28	Denzel Washington, actor, 49 today	

FACTS OF THE WEEK

NEW SUIT FOR SANTA

The name 'Santa Claus' comes from the Dutch Sinter Klaus, short for Sinter Nikolaus or Saint Nicholas. The traditional outfit for Santa was designed by Coca Cola and first appeared in advertisements in 1931. Before this re-vamp Santa's outfit was green!

MOBILE HOME

Marsupials give birth to tiny young that finish developing in a pouch. A baby kangaroo is only 2 centimetres long when it is born. Tiny, blind and hairless, it makes its own way to the safety of its mother's pouch. Once there, it latches onto a teat in the pouch and begins to feed.

BURIED TREASURE

The Egyptians believed that dead people went on to another life. They filled their dead rulers' tombs with things they thought they might need in the next life. These included jewels, food, even pets. This gold mask was found in the tomb of the

JOKE OF THE WEEK

"Why did the vampire baby stop having baby food?"
"He wanted something to get his teeth into!"

QUICK QUIZ

1. How many hours in two days?
2. Who was Queen Victoria's husband?
3. In the nursery rhyme, what were Jack and Jill going up the hill to get?
4. What is a baby deer called?
5. Can an emu fly?
6. What Australian TV programme occurs largely on Ramsey Street?

1. 48 2. Prince Albert
3. A pail of water 4. A fawn
5. No 6. Neighbours

WORD SEARCH

Try and find five Christmas delights in the word search below:

R	C	T	S	A	N	T	A
E	Y	J	W	C	E	O	C
I	N	V	E	W	Z	U	R
N	S	V	E	M	U	T	A
D	H	O	T	L	Y	M	C
E	E	T	S	B	N	M	K
E	H	O	L	L	Y	M	E
R	A	G	J	I	O	M	R

December 2003/January 2004

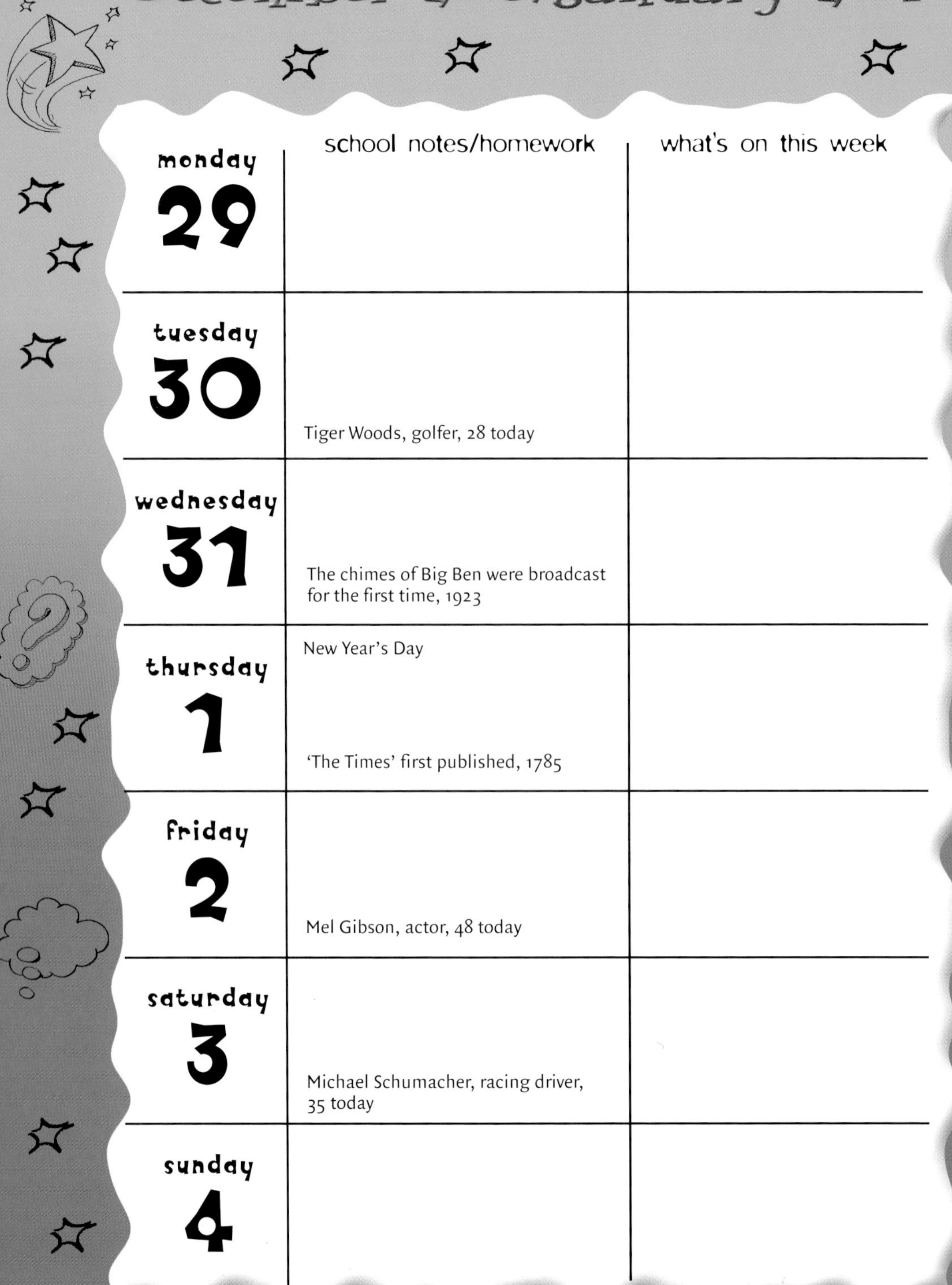

	school notes/homework	what's on this week
monday 29		
tuesday 30	Tiger Woods, golfer, 28 today	
wednesday 31	The chimes of Big Ben were broadcast for the first time, 1923	
thursday 1	New Year's Day 'The Times' first published, 1785	
friday 2	Mel Gibson, actor, 48 today	
saturday 3	Michael Schumacher, racing driver, 35 today	
sunday 4		

FACTS OF THE WEEK

SO ATTRACTIVE

Frigate birds puff up a balloon for their mate. Male frigate birds have a bright-red pouch on their throat. They inflate, or blow up, the pouch as part of their display to attract a female.

THE VERY DEEPEST

The largest, deepest ocean is the Pacific. It covers nearly half of our planet and is almost as big as the other three oceans put together! In places, the Pacific is so deep that the Earth's tallest mountain, Everest, would sink without a trace.

ROMAN MAKE-UP

The Romans painted their faces. The Romans admired pale, smooth skin. Women, and some men, used stick-on patches of cloth called 'splenia' to cover spots, and wore lots of make-up.

JOKE OF THE WEEK

"What's grey, has big ears and a trunk?"
"A mouse on vacation"

QUICK QUIZ

1. What other Australian animal is the wallaby closely related to?
2. Which planet is known as the red planet?
3. Which American president resigned over a scandal known as Watergate?
4. Who was born Elizabeth Alexandra Mary of Windsor?
5. Which tough-guy actor had the nickname Bogey?
6. Are the band Bon Jovi British, Canadian or American?

1. Kangaroo 2. Mars
3. Richard Nixon
4. Queen Elizabeth II
5. Humphrey Bogart 6. American

NAME SCRABBLE

Which superstar singer is hidden in these letters?

HRIAAM ERYAC

MARIAH CAREY

January 2004

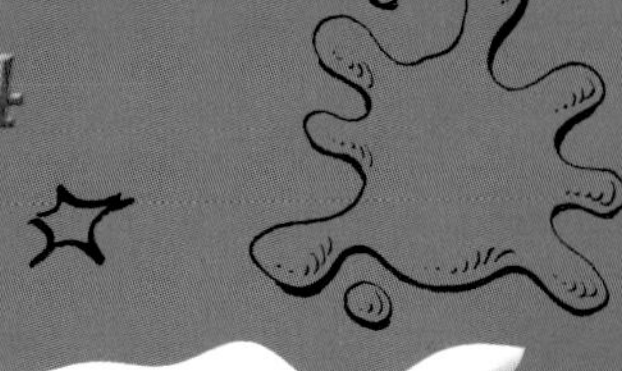

	school notes/homework	what's on this week
monday **5**		
tuesday **6**	Joan of Arc, French heroine, was born 1412	
wednesday **7**		
thursday **8**	Elvis Presley, singer, was born 1935	
friday **9**		
saturday **10**	The London Underground began operating, 1863	
sunday **11**		

FACTS OF THE WEEK

BALANCING TRICK

Emperor penguin dads balance an egg on their feet. They do this to keep the egg off the Antarctic ice, where it would freeze. The female leaves her mate with the egg for the whole two months that it takes to hatch.

'CANDLE IN THE WIND'

Elton John rewrote his song 'Candle in the Wind' for the funeral of Princess Diana in 1997. It became the biggest-selling single ever, with worldwide sales of more than 33 million.

RAINING FISH

Storm winds create strong up-draughts of air over water that can suck up fish and frogs. The animals rain down from the sky, to the surprise of people below!

JOKE OF THE WEEK

"What did the teddy bear say when he was offered dessert?"
"No thanks, I'm stuffed!"

QUICK QUIZ

1. Which American comedy show features Chandler, Monica and Joey?
2. Who was the man behind the cartoon characters Mickey Mouse and Donald Duck?
3. Which cuddly Australian creature lives only on eucalyptus leaves?
4. How many wings does a bee have: two, four or six?
5. What was Winnie the Pooh's favourite food?
6. What is the name of the only Welsh county cricket team?

1. 'Friends' 2. Walt Disney
3. The koala 4. Four
5. Honey 6. Glamorgan

ODD ONE OUT

Which one of the four is the ODD ONE OUT and, why?

SPROUT, POTATO, TOMATO, ONION

TOMATO – all the others are vegetables

January 2004

	school notes/homework	what's on this week
monday 12		
tuesday 13		
wednesday 14	Motorists were required by law to wear seat-belts, 1986	
thursday 15		
friday 16	The Gulf War started with Operation Desert Storm, 1991	
saturday 17	Muhammad Ali, boxing champion, 62 today	
sunday 18		

FACTS OF THE WEEK

REACH FOR THE REPELLENT

Blood-sucking flies bite a person with a certain disease, such as malaria, and suck in a small amount of blood. This contains microscopic germs which cause the disease. As the fly bites another person – the disease is passed on.

SO CLEVER

There are gemstones under the sea. Pearls are made by oysters. If a grain of sand is lodged inside an oyster's shell, it irritates its soft body. The oyster coats the sand with a substance called nacre, over the years, more nacre builds up and the pearl gets bigger.

ANTARCTIC DISASTER

Captain Robert Scott's second expedition to reach the South Pole ended in tragedy. When his team finally reached the South Pole on January 18, 1912, they found that a Norwegian team had arrived there one month earlier. Scott and his men died from hunger and the cold on the way home.

JOKE OF THE WEEK

"What kind of beans can't grow in a garden?"

"Jelly Beans"

QUICK QUIZ

1. What was the name of Fred Flintstone's next door neighbour and buddy?
2. Which John has been Minister for Transport and is nicknamed 'Two Jags'?
3. In which country are the native people called Maoris?
4. Beetle, Golf and Polo are all made by which motor manufacturer?
5. Who was the youngest daughter of Henry VIII?
6. Which ancient king had a round table?

1. Barney Rubble 2. John Prescott 3. New Zealand 4. Volkswagen (VW) 5. Elizabeth I 6. King Arthur

PROVERBIAL PUZZLE

In the proverb, what do too many cooks spoil?

The broth

January 2004

	school notes/homework	what's on this week
monday **19**	The first German Zeppelins raided England, 1915	
tuesday **20**		
wednesday **21**	Concorde makes its 1st supersonic commercial flight, 1976	
thursday **22**	An earthquake in China kills 830,000 people, 1556	
friday **23**		
saturday **24**		
sunday **25**	Robert Burns, poet, was born 1759	

FACTS OF THE WEEK

SUPERSTAR

American actor Brad Pitt is one of the most popular film stars of modern times. Newspapers often encourage readers to think that the lives of such superstars are as dramatic as the mythical characters they portray on screen.

DEEP SEA DIVER

In 1960, two men inside the diving vehicle 'Trieste' descended more than 10 kilometres into the Marianas Trench, the deepest part of the Pacific Ocean. The 'Trieste' was also use to explore the wreck of the Titanic and reclaim some of her contents.

BEHEADED!

Throughout history, people have sometimes turned against their king. Charles I was king of England and Scotland in the 1600s. Although he lost a civil war in Britain, Charles still refused to give up his powers. He was finally beheaded in London on January 31, 1649.

JOKE OF THE WEEK

"Why did the golfer wear two sets of pants?"
"In case he got a whole in one!"

QUICK QUIZ

1. What animal is the book 'Black Beauty' about?
2. Which boy wizard has stormed to fame in a series of books?
3. What is the name given to a female pig?
4. Which bird comes in the varieties tawny and barn?
5. How many grammes in a kilogram?
6. Which city did The Beatles come from?

1. A horse 2. Harry Potter
3. Sow 4. Owl
5. 1000 6. Liverpool

NAME SCRAMBLE

Which famous home is hidden in the scramble below?

CIGMAHNKUB CELAAP

BUCKINGHAM PALACE

January/February 2004

	school notes/homework	what's on this week
monday **26**		
tuesday **27**	John Logie Baird demonstrated television, 1926	
wednesday **28**	King Henry VIII died 1547	
thursday **29**		
friday **30**	The Beatles performed together for the last time, 1969	
saturday **31**		
sunday **1**		

FACTS OF THE WEEK

LITTLE CHANGE

Roman combs were made from bone, ivory or wood. Like combs today, they were designed to smooth and untangle hair, and were sometimes worn as hair ornaments. But they had another, less pleasant, purpose – they were used for combing out all the little nits and lice!

THE SMALLEST AND THE TALLEST

One of the smallest mammals is a bat. It is called Kitti's hog-nosed bat and is less than 2 centimetres long – about the same size as a bumble bee. The tallest mammal is the giraffe measuring a mighty 5.5 metres high.

CHANGING SHAPE

The Moon seems to change shape from day to day. It takes 28.73 days to pass through all these changes, which we call phases. Sometimes we see just a tiny slice of the Moon – this is because the rest of the Moon is in darkness.

JOKE OF THE WEEK

"What did the Pacific Ocean say to the Atlantic Ocean?"
"Nothing. It just waved."

QUICK QUIZ

1. How many teams are relegated from the Premiership every year?
2. With which classical musical instrument is Nigel Kennedy associated?
3. What country is bordered by China and the former USSR?
4. What phone number is usually dialled for the emergency services in Britain?
5. What structure would Clark Kent visit to change into Superman?
6. What frontier wall was built in AD122?

1. Three 2. The violin
3. Mongolia 4. 999
5. A telephone box
6. Hadrian's Wall

ODD ONE OUT

Which famous pop star is hidden in these letters?

IEOBRB SAMLWLII

ROBBIE WILLIAMS

February 2004

	school notes/homework	what's on this week
monday 2		
tuesday 3	The Soviet spacecraft Luna 9 reached the Moon, 1966	
wednesday 4		
thursday 5		
friday 6	Queen Elizabeth II succeeded to the throne, 1952	
saturday 7	Charles Dickens, author, was born 1812	
sunday 8	Mary Queen of Scots was beheaded, 1587	

FACTS OF THE WEEK

MEDIEVAL FIGHTING

Jousting was introduced because so many knights were being killed or wounded during tournaments. Jousting was a fight between two knights on horseback. Each knight tried to win by knocking the other off his horse.

HIDDEN TREASURES

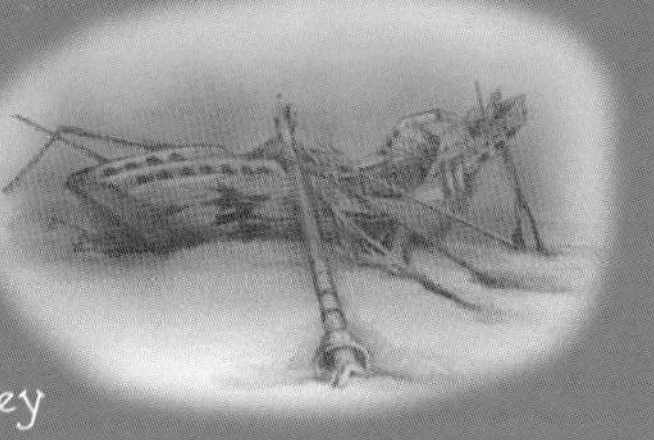

There is treasure lying under the sea. Over the centuries, many ships sunk in storms or hit reefs. They include pirate ships loaded with stolen booty. The bed of the Caribbean Sea is littered with the remains of Spanish galleons, many of which still hold treasure!

THE BIG APPLE

Broadway in New York is America's theatreland – the equivalent of London's West End – and is the place were British and American actors most want to perform. If a play transfers to Broadway from a West End theatre, it is considered a success.

JOKE OF THE WEEK

"Why do birds fly south in the winter?"
"Because it's too far to walk!"

QUICK QUIZ

1. Which king was alleged to have commanded the sea to retreat?
2. How do you feel if you are 'tickled pink'?
3. Who was Sherlock Holmes's faithful assistant?
4. Which land animal is the fastest runner?
5. What fruit is used to make wine?
6. Which British and French plane is the only supersonic airliner in service?

1. King Canute 2. Very happy
3. Doctor Watson
4. The cheetah 5. Grapes
6. Concorde

WORD SEARCH

Try and find five boys or girls names in the word search below

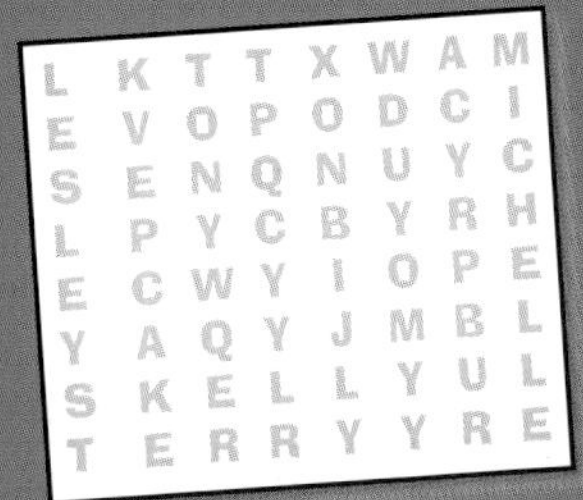

L	K	T	T	X	W	A	M
E	V	O	P	O	D	C	I
S	E	N	Q	N	U	Y	C
L	P	Y	C	B	Y	R	H
E	C	W	Y	I	O	P	E
Y	A	Q	Y	J	M	B	L
S	K	E	L	L	Y	U	L
T	E	R	R	Y	Y	R	E

February 2004

	school notes/homework	what's on this week
monday 9		
tuesday 10		
wednesday 11	Jennifer Aniston, actress, 35 today	
thursday 12	Abraham Lincoln, former US president, was born 1809	
friday 13	Robbie Williams, singer 30 today	
saturday 14	Kevin Keegan, former England footballer and manager, 53 today	
sunday 15	Galileo, astronomer, was born 1564	

FACTS OF THE WEEK

DON'T TRY THIS AT HOME

Sauropod dinosaurs may have swallowed pebbles - on purpose! Their peglike teeth could only rake in plant food, not chew it. Pebbles and stones gulped into the stomach helped to grind and crush the food.

EARLY ROMANCE

The Romans invented Valentine's Day, but called it Lupercalia. Boys picked a girl's name from a hat, and she was meant to be their girlfriend for the year! Childhood was short for a Roman girl. Roman law allowed girls to get married at 12 years old.

DRAMATIC THEATRE

The Colosseum was a vast amphitheatre in Rome, Italy. Ancient Romans flocked there - it held up to 50,000 spectators - to watch gladiators fighting each other or wild animals. There was even a mock sea battle in the arena, which was flooded for the occasion.

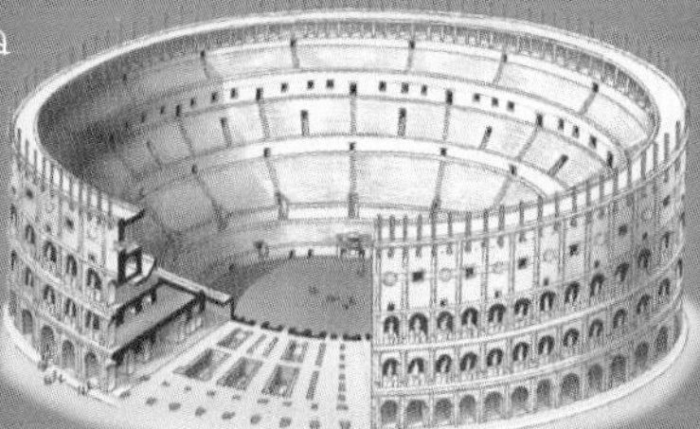

JOKE OF THE WEEK

"What is "out of bounds"?"
"An exhausted kangaroo!"

QUICK QUIZ

1. In what part of London is the Millennium Dome situated?
2. What sort of animal was often killed by a harpoon?
3. What do the initials NHS stand for?
4. Is A6 paper bigger than A5?
5. What sort of animal is a pug?
6. Does the rice dish risotto come from India, Wales or Italy?

1. Greenwich 2. A whale
3. National Health Service
4. No, it is half the size of A5
5. A dog 6. Italy

COCKNEY LINGO

What words do the following Cockney Rhymes describe?

(a) Apples and pears (b) North and south (c) Plates of meat (d) Dog and bone (e) Trouble and strife

(a) stairs (b) mouth (c) feet
(d) phone (e) wife

February 2004

	school notes/homework	what's on this week
monday **16**		
tuesday **17**	Tutankhamen's tomb was opened at Luxor, Egypt, 1923	
wednesday **18**	John Travolta, actor, 50 today	
thursday **19**	Thomas Edison patented the phonograph, 1878	
friday **20**		
saturday **21**	Charlotte Church, singer, 18 today	
sunday **22**	The first British cinema to be built opened in Lancashire, 1906	

FACTS OF THE WEEK

A TERRIBLE END

In the 1420s a young French girl called Joan of Arc led the French army against the English, who had surrounded the city of Orléans. After ten days the English were defeated. Joan was later captured, accused of being a witch, and burned to death.

ESSENTIAL EQUIPMENT

Divers have a spare pair of lungs. Scuba divers wear special breathing apparatus called 'aqua lungs'. French divers, Jacques Cousteau and Emile Gagnan, came up with the idea of a portable oxygen supply.

THE WONDER DRUG TO TREAT INFECTIONS

In 1928 Alexander Fleming found that penicillin mould, killed bacteria – a chance discovery that led to the first antibiotic, penicillin. It is prescribed by doctors to treat all sorts of infections.

JOKE OF THE WEEK

"What followed the dinosaur?"
"It's tail!"

QUICK QUIZ

1. What was mead: a type of bread, an alcoholic drink, a simple hut?
2. What is the past tense of the word creep?
3. What do the initials MP stand for?
4. Do conifers produce flowers?
5. What is a baby elephant called?
6. Does hot air travel up or down?

1. An alcoholic drink 2. Crept 3. Member of Parliament or Military Police 4. No 5. Calf 6. Up

WORD SCRAMBLE

Scrambled in the mix-up below is something that travels faster than the speed of sound!

CNDOCROE

CONCORDE

February 2004

	school notes/homework	what's on this week
monday 23		
tuesday 24		
wednesday 25		
thursday 26	The first £1 note was issued by the Bank of England, 1797	
friday 27	The Gulf War ended, 1991	
saturday 28		
sunday 29	This day only occurs once every four years – a leap year!	

FACTS OF THE WEEK

EARLY BIRD

Birds first appeared about 150 million years ago. It is possible that over millions of years certain small, meat-eating dinosaurs called raptors developed feathers. Slowly their arms became wings. Gradually they evolved into the very first birds.

FOR THE FUTURE

The planned Freedom Ship will resemble a floating city. It will be one of the first ocean cities, with apartments, shopping centres, a school and a hospital. The people who live on Freedom will circle the Earth once every two years. By following the Sun, they will live in constant summertime!

MIRACLE BABY

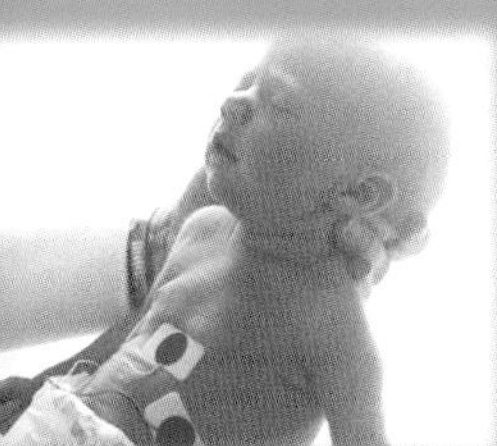

Louise Brown, born in 1978, was the first 'test-tube' baby. She was conceived outside her mothers's body, and the fertilized egg was then implanted in her mothers's womb to continue growing normally.

JOKE OF THE WEEK

"How was the Roman Empire cut in half?"
"With a pair of Caesars!"

QUICK QUIZ

1. What element has the chemical symbol O?
2. Who was the shy dwarf in the story of Snow White?
3. Which Australian soap started the careers of Jason Donovan and Kylie Minogue?
4. Which science fiction film starred Ewan McGregor as a Jedi Knight?
5. How do Americans spell grey?
6. What two paint colours would you mix to make purple?

1. Oxygen 2. Bashful
3. Neighbours 4. Star Wars
Episode 1: The Phantom Menac
5. Gray
6. Red and blue

PROVERBIAL PUZZLE

In the proverb, red sky at night is shepherd's delight, but red sky in the morning is what?

Shepherd's warning

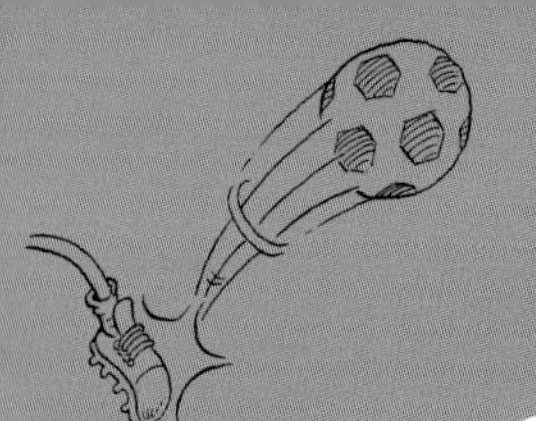

March 2004

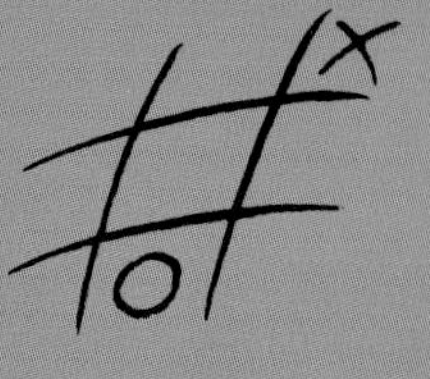

	school notes/homework	what's on this week
monday 1	St David's Day The Soviet spacecraft Venus touched down on the planet Venus, 1966	
tuesday 2		
wednesday 3	Ronan Keating, singer, 27 today	
thursday 4		
friday 5		
saturday 6	Shaquille O'Neal, basketballer, 32 today	
sunday 7	The first radio-telephone link was established between New York and London, 1926	

FACTS OF THE WEEK

PRAYERS BEFORE DINNER

One of the most powerful insect predators is the preying mantis. It is also called the praying mantis since it holds its front legs folded, like a person with hands together in prayer. But the front legs have sharp spines which snap together to grab caterpillars, moths and similar food.

LOSING COUNT

The worlds's oldest person is usually a woman aged between 110 and 120. Only one person in five over 100 is a man. Many claims for 'oldest person' are false. In 1933 a Chinese man was reported to have died at the age of 233!

ANCIENT MONUMENT

Stonehenge is the most famous ancient monument in Britain. It was built between about 2950 and 1500BC. The huge stones were put up in stages, in three circles that made a giant calendar which was used to fix days for religious ceremonies.

JOKE OF THE WEEK

"How do porcupines play leapfrog?"

"Very carefully"

QUICK QUIZ

1. Which TV show features Del Boy and Rodney Trotter?
2. What is the name of Sunderland Football Club's stadium?
3. Which famous drummer's real name is Richard Starkey?
4. Jim Henson provided the puppets for which famous children's show?
5. If you serve a double fault, what sport are you playing?
6. What word means a small downpour of rain and also a bathroom spraying device?

1. Only Fools and Horses
2. The Stadium of Light
3. Ringo Starr 4. The Muppets
5. Tennis 6. Shower

NAME SCRAMBLE

Which tall London building is hiding in the scramble below?

RYNAAC FHARW

CANARY WHARF

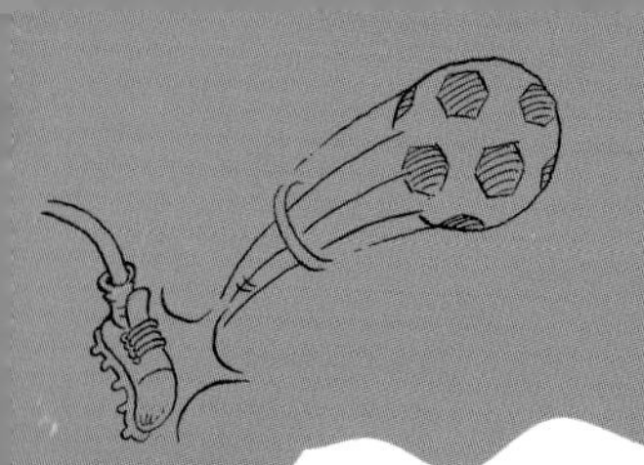

March 2004

	school notes/homework	what's on this week
monday 8		
tuesday 9	Yuri Gagarin, first man in space, was born 1934	
wednesday 10	Prince Edward 40 today	
thursday 11	Alexander Graham Bell made the first telephone call, 1876	
friday 12	A 30 mph (48 km/h) speed limit in built-up areas was imposed on cars, 1935	
saturday 13	William Herschel discovered the planet Uranus, 1781	
sunday 14	Michael Caine, actor, 71 today	

FACTS OF THE WEEK

SPOOKY HAPPENINGS

Many castles are said to be haunted by the ghosts of people who died within their walls. Edward II of England was murdered in his cell at Berkeley Castle, and visitors to the castle say they can hear the screams of the murdered Edward at night.

KILLING FOR SPORT

Roman gladiators fought wild beasts, as well as each other. Fierce wild animals were brought from distant parts of the Roman empire to be killed by gladiators in the arenas in Rome. So many lions were taken from North Africa that they became extinct there.

MYTHS AND LEGENDS

Mermaids lured sailors to their deaths on the rocks. Mythical mermaids were said to be half-woman, half-fish. Folklore tells how the mermaids confused sailors with their beautiful singing – with the result that their ships were wrecked on the rocks.

JOKE OF THE WEEK

"What is a volcano?"
"A mountain with hiccups!"

QUICK QUIZ

1. What famous London church was founded by Edward in 1052?
2. How many days did it take for Phileas Fogg to travel around the Earth?
3. How many people would you find in a duet?
4. How does a python kill its prey?
5. What name is given to a female dog?
6. What is 50% of 212?

1. Westminster Abbey
2. 80 days 3. Two
4. It crushes them 5. Bitch
6. 106

WHO IS SHE?

She is my father's niece, my uncle's daughter, and my cousin's sister. Who is she?

My cousin

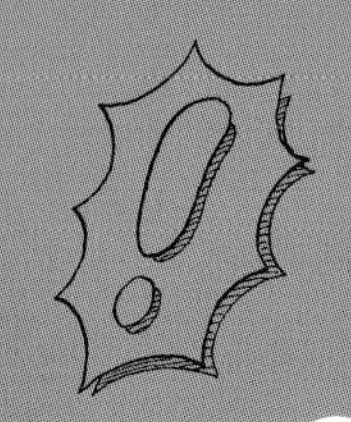

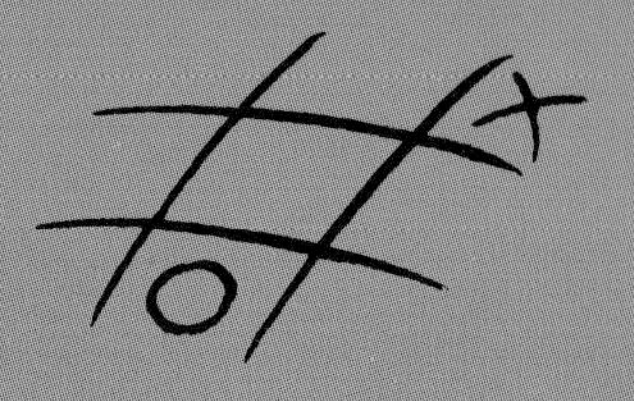

March 2004

	school notes/homework	what's on this week
monday **15**		
tuesday **16**	The first football cup final was played, Kensington Oval, 1872	
wednesday **17**	St Patrick's Day	
thursday **18**	The planet Pluto was discovered, 1930	
friday **19**	Bruce Willis, actor, 49 today	
saturday **20**		
sunday **21**		

FACTS OF THE WEEK

WRAPPED IN LAYERS

The Earth is wrapped in layers of gases called the atmosphere. The weather takes place in the lowest layer, the troposphere. The layer above is the stratosphere. The mesosphere is the middle layer and above it is the thermosphere. The exosphere is about 700 kilometres above your head!

WITCHCRAFT

Despite their advanced technology, Romans believed that illness was caused by witchcraft. To find a cure, they gave presents to the witch, begging her to remove the spell, or made a special visit to a temple, to ask the gods to make them better.

ELEMENTARY MY DEAR WATSON

The most famous detective in literature is Sherlock Holmes. Frequently mistaken by readers for a real person, Holmes and his friend Dr Watson first appeared in Arthur Conan Doyle's story 'A Study In Scarlet'ß in 1887.

JOKE OF THE WEEK

"Why did the silly kid stand on his head?"
"His feet were tired!"

QUICK QUIZ

1. Does the polar bear live in the Arctic or Antarctic?
2. What creature can contain a natural pearl inside its shell?
3. Which elephant could fly?
4. Which country won the 1998 football World Cup?
5. Which sisters were responsible for classics of English literature including 'Wuthering Heights'?
6. What type of appliance is the name Dyson associated with?

1. The Arctic 2. An oyster
3. Dumbo 4. France
5. The Brontës
6. Vacuum cleaner

CONUNDRUM

As I was going to St Ives, I met a man with seven wives, each wife had seven sacks, each sack had seven cats, each cat had seven kits; Kits, cats, sacks and wives, How many were going to St Ives?

One, all the others were going back!

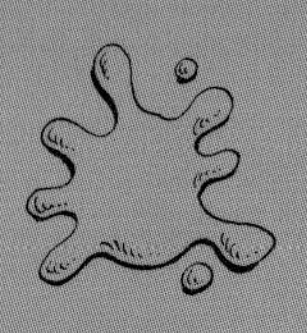

March 2004

	school notes/homework	what's on this week
monday 22	The English Football League was founded, 1888	
tuesday 23	Adolf Hitler became dictator of Germany, 1933	
wednesday 24	At the Boat Race, Oxford and Cambridge dead-heated, 1877	
thursday 25	Elton John, songwriter, 57 today	
friday 26	Driving tests were introduced in Britain, 1934	
saturday 27		
sunday 28		

FACTS OF THE WEEK

TOP OF THE POPS

Dolphins and whales sing songs to communicate. The noisiest is the humpback whale, whose wailing noises can be heard for hundreds of kilometres. The sweetest is the beluga – nicknamed the 'sea canary'. Songs are used to attract a mate, or just to keep track of each other.

ALL DRIED UP

The driest place on Earth is the Atacama Desert in Chile, South America. Intervals between showers may be as long as 100 years, and in some areas it has not rained for more than 400 years!

WHAT THE DICKENS

Charles Dickens (1812–70) was one of the most popular novelists of all time. His books such as 'A Christmas Carol' and 'Oliver Twist' are full of memorable characters, humour and sadness.

JOKE OF THE WEEK

"Who invented fractions?"

"Henry the 1/8!"

QUICK QUIZ

1. Were the Velvet Underground a band, a terrorist group or a group of modern artists?
2. What is measured in centigrade?
3. Which monarch reigned longest in Britain?
4. In what year did Japan bomb Pearl Harbor?
5. What is the meaning of the initials UFO?
6. What type of animal are spaniels and beagles?

1. A band 2. Temperature
3. Queen Victoria 4. 1941
5. Unidentified Flying Object
6. Dogs

WORD SEARCH

Find the five football clubs hidden below.

T	H	U	W	S	M	O	A
A	E	V	E	R	T	O	N
R	E	Q	S	K	U	E	F
S	C	W	T	I	I	S	P
E	G	G	H	X	R	P	L
N	N	S	A	V	H	U	E
A	B	C	M	P	I	R	H
L	E	E	D	S	O	S	W

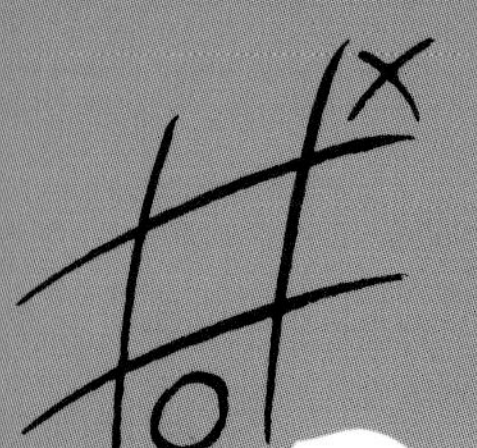

March/April 2004

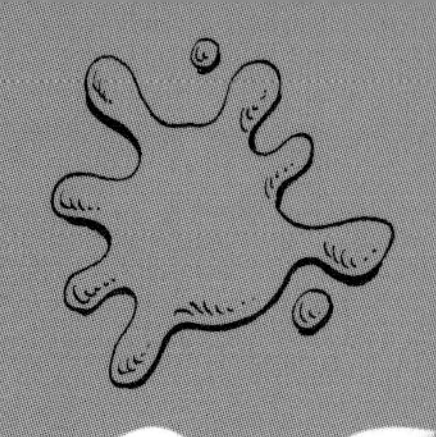

	school notes/homework	what's on this week
monday 29		
tuesday 30	Vincent van Gogh, painter, was born 1853	
wednesday 31	Ewan McGregor, actor, 33 today	
thursday 1		
friday 2	Argentina invaded and occupied the Falklands, 1982	
saturday 3	Eddie Murphy, actor, 44 today	
sunday 4		

FACTS OF THE WEEK

GEORGE AND THE DRAGON

The legend of St George tells how the brave knight killed a fierce dragon. The dragon was terrorizing the people of Lydia. St George arrived and said he would kill their dragon if they became Christians like him. Thousands accepted his offer, and George killed the dragon.

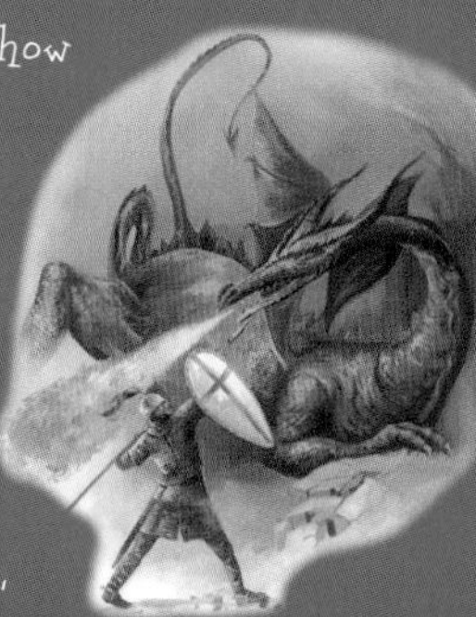

IN ANCIENT ROME

Roman theatres were huge, well-built structures. One of the best-preserved is at Orange, in France. It has seats for almost 10,000 people. It was so cleverly designed that the audience could hear the actors, even from the back row.

BESTSELLING AUTHOR

The biggest-selling writer ever is Agatha Christie (1890–1976). Her 78 crime stories, featuring detectives Hercule Poirot and Miss Marple, have been translated into more than 44 languages. Many have been made into plays.

JOKE OF THE WEEK

"Who was the first underwater spy?"
"James Pond!"

QUICK QUIZ

1. What are the two types of squirrel which live in Britain?
2. Do hippos eat fish?
3. What mammal feeds entirely on ants?
4. What covers more than two thirds of the world's surface?
5. How many times does 9 go into 81?
6. When water becomes ice, does it expand or contract?

1. Red and grey squirrel
2. No 3. Anteater
4. Water 5. Nine 6. Expand

CAN YOU GUESS?

What are the five largest countries in the world?

Russia, Canada, China, United States, Brazil

April 2004

	school notes/homework	what's on this week
monday **5**		
tuesday **6**	George Washington was elected first president of the USA, 1789	
wednesday **7**		
thursday **8**		
friday **9**	Robbie Fowler, footballer, 29 today	
saturday **10**	Bananas first on sale in London, 1633	
sunday **11**		

FACTS OF THE WEEK

MINOTAUR

The Minotaur was a monster of ancient Greek legend. It had the body of a man, but the head, horns, and tail of a bull, and it fed on human flesh. The Minotaur was kept beneath the palace of King Minos of Crete and was eventually killed by the hero-prince Theseus.

ANCIENT CULTURE

The Roma people – sometimes called 'Gypsies' – have preserved their ancient nomadic way of life for hundreds of years, along with their own customs. Originally from India, Roma now live in many parts of Europe and northern Africa.

CINEMATOGRAPHE

The Lumiere brothers invented the 'cinematographe', a device that combines the camera and the projector. By showing numerous pictures one after the other they could create the illusion of motion.

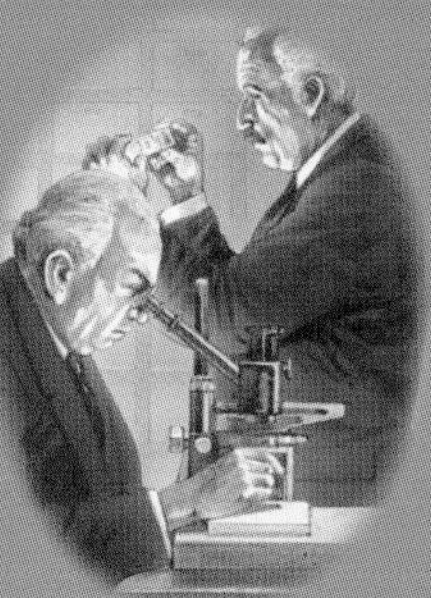

JOKE OF THE WEEK

"What is hairy and coughs?"

"A coconut with a cold!"

QUICK QUIZ

1. What happened in space on July 20, 1969?
2. As a fraction, how much is 25% of something?
3. In what decade is the comedy drama 'The Grimleys set'?
4. In snooker, how many points is the green ball worth?
5. Actor Tony Booth is the father of which politician's wife?
6. In what decade was the first 'Star Wars' film released?

1. Man landed on the Moon 2. ¼ 3. The 1970s 4. Three 5. Tony Blair 6. The 1970s

ODD ONE OUT

Which of these singers is the odd one out?

Madonna, Michael Jackson, Britney Spears, Robbie Williams

Robbie Williams, All the others are American.

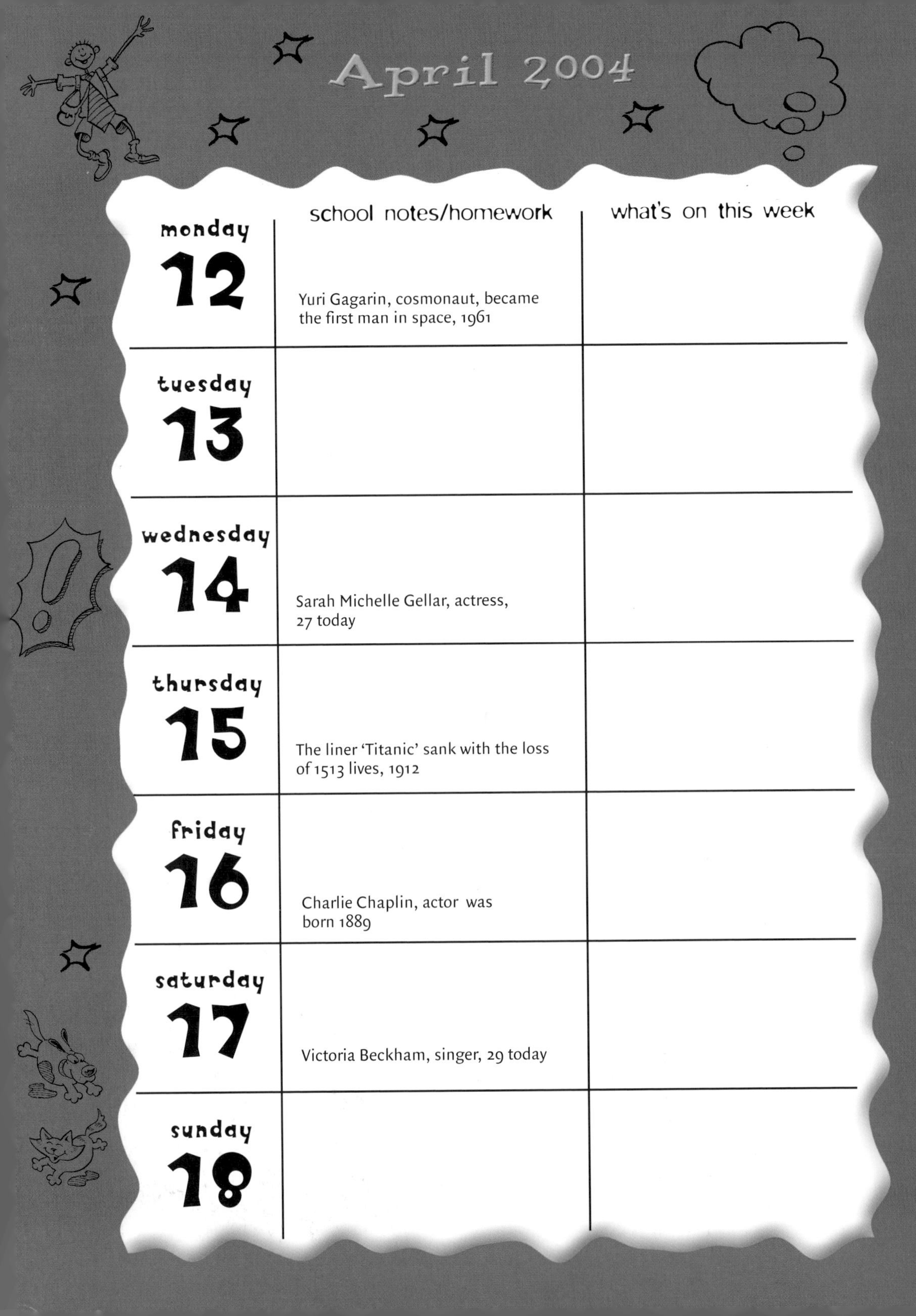

April 2004

	school notes/homework	what's on this week
monday 12	Yuri Gagarin, cosmonaut, became the first man in space, 1961	
tuesday 13		
wednesday 14	Sarah Michelle Gellar, actress, 27 today	
thursday 15	The liner 'Titanic' sank with the loss of 1513 lives, 1912	
friday 16	Charlie Chaplin, actor was born 1889	
saturday 17	Victoria Beckham, singer, 29 today	
sunday 18		

FACTS OF THE WEEK

PAINTBALL BATTLE

The bombardier beetle squirts out a spray of horrible liquid from its rear end, almost like a small spray-gun! This startles and stings the attacker and gives the small beetle time to escape.

BUILT BY THE CONQUEROR

English kings and queens have lived at Windsor Castle since William the Conqueror began building it more than 900 years ago. William's original castle consisted of a wooden fort. The first stone buildings were added in the 1100s.

ALL IN THE DOTS

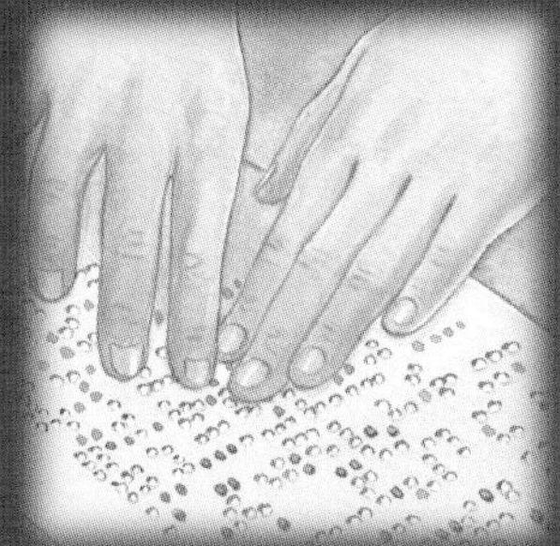

Braille is a raised-dot alphabet used by blind people. It is read by running the fingertips over the dots, or bumps. Braille was invented by a blind French teenager named Louis Braille in the 1820s.

JOKE OF THE WEEK

"What do you call a foreign body in a chip pan?"
"An Unidentified Frying Object!"

QUICK QUIZ

1. What is agricultural land used for?
2. Pudding Lane in London was the starting point for which London disaster?
3. What word is a writing instrument and a fenced in area to hold sheep?
4. What substance transports oxygen and nutrients around the body?
5. Does a giraffe have more, less or the same number of neck bones as humans?
6. If someone was examining your cranium, what part of your body would they be looking at?

1. Farming 2. The Great Fire of London 3. Pen 4. Blood 5. The same number 6. Head

WORD SCRAMBLE

Unscramble the letters to find three famous cities

LIBREN, SPAIR, BREENMOUL,

BERLIN, PARIS, MELBOURNE

April 2004

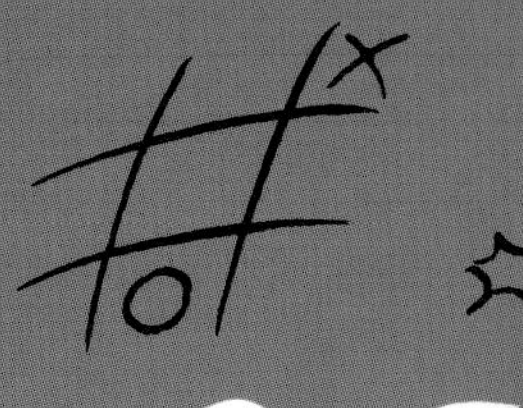

	school notes/homework	what's on this week
monday 19		
tuesday 20		
wednesday 21	Queen Elizabeth II, 78 today	
thursday 22		
friday 23	St George's Day William Shakespeare, playwright, was born 1564	
saturday 24		
sunday 25		

FACTS OF THE WEEK

HURRICANE FORCE

A hurricane is a destructive storm which gathers over a warm part of the ocean. Water evaporating from the ocean forms a vast cloud. As cool air rushes in below the cloud, it turns like a huge spinning wheel. The centre of the hurricane (the eye) is completely still.

OSTRICH DINOSAUR

Struthiomimus was one of the fastest of all the dinosaurs. It was more than 2 metres tall and 4 metres long. It had very long back legs and large clawed feet, like an ostrich. It could probably run at more than 70 kilometres per hour.

WARRIORS FROM THE EAST

Warrier knights in Japan in the Middle Ages were known as Samurai. A long curving sword was a samurai warrior's most treasured possession. Samurai warriors wore armour on the bodies, arms and legs, a helmet and often a crest made up of a pair of horns.

JOKE OF THE WEEK

"Why did the lazy man want a job in a bakery?"

"So he could loaf around!"

QUICK QUIZ

1. What doctor had a phone box for a time machine?
2. What standard facial feature is missing from the Mona Lisa painting?
3. On which Japanese city was the first atom bomb dropped?
4. In which fairytale did a girl eat the porridge of the three bears?
5. What part of a cow is squeezed to release milk?
6. Is a kilogram more or less than two pounds?

1. Dr Who 2. Eyebrows
3. Hiroshima 4. Goldilocks
5. The udder 6. More

NUMBER PUZZLE

Multiply the number of legs on a spider by the number of blind mice in the song. Take away the number of the dwarves in Snow White. What is your answer?

17. 8 (legs on a spider x 3 (blind mice) = 24-7 (dwarves) = 17

April/May 2004

	school notes/homework	what's on this week
monday 26	Leonardo da Vinci, painter and sculptor, was born 1452	
tuesday 27	London Zoo first opened, 1828	
wednesday 28	The crew of HMS 'Bounty' mutinied, 1789	
thursday 29	Michelle Pfeiffer, actress, 47 today	
friday 30		
saturday 1		
sunday 2	David Beckham, footballer, 29 today	

FACTS OF THE WEEK

BATHTIME PETS

Sponges are animals! They are very simple creatures that filter food from sea water. The natural sponge that you might use in the bath is a long-dead, dried-out sponge.

EARLY CHRISTIANITY

Some of the world's first Christians lived in Rome. But until AD313 Christianity was banned in the Roman Empire. Christians met secretly in underground passages called catacombs, to say prayers and hold services. They also used the catacombs as a burial place.

MAKING MUSIC

The guitar's origins go back to ancient Egypt, but the shape of the Spanish acoustic guitar, shown here, dates from the 1800s. Most guitars have 6 strings, but some have 12. Guitars used by ex-rock stars sell for huge sums of money.

QUICK QUIZ

1. At room temperature, is helium a gas, a liquid or a solid?

2. According to the proverb, a bird in the hand is worth how many in the bush?

3. What was the name of the airships which bombed London in 1915?

4. In which country is Seville?

5. Which football team plays at Stamford Bridge?

6. In what decade did the Gulf War occur?

1. A gas 2. Two
3. Zeppelins 4. Spain
5. Chelsea 6. The 1990s

ODD ONE OUT

Which of the following countries is the odd one out and why?

INDIA, JAPAN, KENYA, CHINA

KENYA – All the others are countries in Asia.

JOKE OF THE WEEK

"Why are graveyards so noisy?"
"Because of all the coffin!"

May 2004

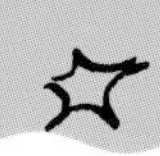

	school notes/homework	what's on this week
monday **3**		
tuesday **4**	The first Derby was run at Epsom, 1780	
wednesday **5**	Tony Blair, prime minister, 49 today	
thursday **6**	Peter Tchaikovsky, composer, was born 1840	
friday **7**		
saturday **8**	Germany signed the surrender to end World War II in Europe, 1945	
sunday **9**	Britain's first launderette opened, London, 1949	

FACTS OF THE WEEK

SAVE THE PLANET!

We can make materials last longer by recycling them. Metal, glass and plastic are thrown away after they have been used, buried in tips and never used again. Today more people recycle materials. This means sending them back to factories to be used again.

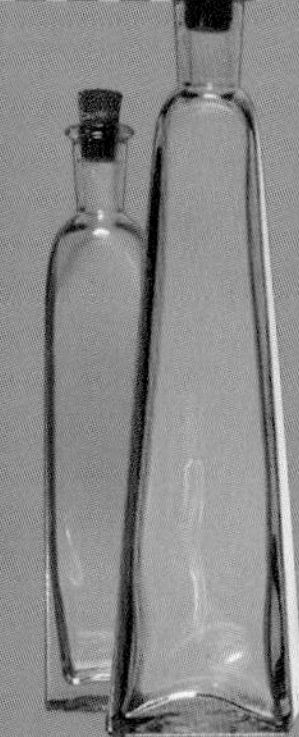

WELL ARMED

The narwhal has a horn like a unicorn's. This Arctic whale has a long, twirly tooth which measures about 3 metres long and spirals out of its head. The males use their tusks as a weapon when they are fighting over females.

RIP VAN WINKLE

In the traditional tale, Rip Van Winkle falls into a deep sleep for 20 years. When he finally wakes up, he can't understand why the world is so different.

JOKE OF THE WEEK

"What lights up a football stadium?"
"A football match!"

QUICK QUIZ

1. Which American president was shot dead in a theatre in 1865?
2. Which country's flag is known as the star-spangled banner?
3. What type of instrument is a Fender Stratocaster?
4. In what sport would you use parallel bars?
5. What is the name given to an elephant's long pointed teeth?
6. Who was the one-legged pirate in the adventure story 'Treasure Island'?

1. Abraham Lincoln 2. The United States 3. An electric guitar 4. Gymnastics 5. Tusks 6. Long John Silver

TAKE FIVE

Name the last five different countries to win the football World Cup

Brazil, France, West Germany, Argentina, Italy

	school notes/homework	what's on this week
monday 10	Bono, singer, 43 today	
tuesday 11		
wednesday 12	Florence Nightingale, heroine nurse, was born, 1820	
thursday 13	The United States declared war on Mexico, 1846	
friday 14	1st passenger flight in an airplane, 1908	
saturday 15		
sunday 16	The first Academy Awards were presented, Hollywood, 1929	

FACTS OF THE WEEK

NO DRIFTING OFF

Sea otters anchor themselves when they sleep. These playful creatures live off the Pacific coast among huge forests of giant seaweed called kelp. When they take a snooze, they wrap a strand of kelp around their body to stop them being washed out to sea.

POISONED QUEEN

Cleopatra was queen of ancient Egypt when the country was under the control of the Romans. She was a very ambitious and determined queen. According to legend, Cleopatra killed herself by letting a poisonous snake bite her arm.

SAVING THE TREES

For many New Age sympathizers, protecting the natural environment from destruction has become a spiritual quest. They hold ceremonies to celebrate nature's beauty, and campaign to save fragile environments, such as rainforests, from harm.

JOKE OF THE WEEK

"What starts with T, ends with T, and is filled with T?"
"A teapot!"

QUICK QUIZ

1. A peregrine falcon can reach 270 km/h in a dive – true or false?

2. What is the most common element in the Earth's atmosphere?

3. What name was given to the American missions to the Moon?

4. Oslo is the capital of which Scandinavian country?

5. How many atom bombs have been dropped?

6. What word, starting with f, do Americans use for the Autumn season?

1. True 2. Nitrogen
3. Apollo 4. Norway
5. Two 6. Fall

WORD SEARCH

Can you find five African animals hiding amongst the letters below?

May 2004

	school notes/homework	what's on this week
monday 17		
tuesday 18		
wednesday 19	The Spanish Armada set sail from Lisbon, 1588	
thursday 20	Amelia Earhart was the first woman to fly solo across the Atlantic, 1932	
friday 21		
saturday 22	Sir Arthur Conan Doyle, author, was born 1859	
sunday 23		

FACTS OF THE WEEK

IVANHOE

Ivanhoe was a medieval knight who lived in the time of Richard the Lionheart. He is the hero of a historical book called 'Ivanhoe', written by the Scottish novelist Sir Walter Scott in the 1800s, and describes the conflict between the Saxon people and their Norman conquerors.

SIGNS OF FAITH

Some Jewish men wear special clothes as a sign of their faith. The kippah (or yarmulke) is a little cap that covers the crown of the head and is worn as a mark of respect for God. For praying, Jewish men may wear a tallit, or shawl.

THE LOUVRE

The Louvre in Paris contains one of the world's greatest art collections. Once a royal palace, it was extended in the 17th century to house the growing royal collection. In 1989 it was given a new, ultramodern entrance under a pyramid.

JOKE OF THE WEEK

"What do whales eat?"
"Fish and ships"

QUICK QUIZ

1. When were the Olympic Games held in Barcelona?
2. Which Australian entertainer hosts a show about animal hospitals?
3. What country did the Germans invade to start World War II?
4. In which tales would you find Friar Tuck and Maid Marian?
5. How many kidneys does the human body normally contain?
6. If you received £4 pocket money a week, how many weeks would you have to save up to reach £36?

1. 1996 2. Rolf Harris
3. Poland 4. Robin Hood
5. Two 6. Nine

NUMBER PUZZLE

Which number should replace the question mark?

8	7	6	9	?
3	5	4	6	5
5	2	2	3	9

Answer: 14

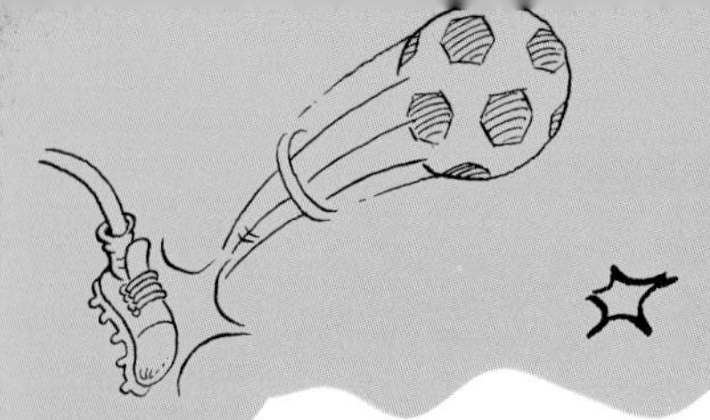

May 2004

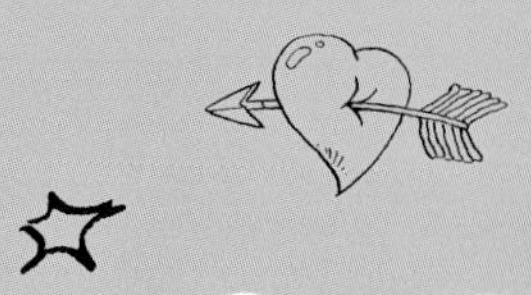

	school notes/homework	what's on this week
monday **24**	Queen Victoria was born 1819	
tuesday **25**	Captain Cook sailed on his first voyage, 1768	
wednesday **26**		
thursday **27**	Cilla Black, TV presenter, 61 today	
friday **28**		
saturday **29**	Sir Edmund Hillary and Sherpa Tenzing reached the summit of Mount Everest, 1953	
sunday **30**	Joan of Arc died at the stake, 1431	

FACTS OF THE WEEK

IN THE PINK

Walruses seem to change colour! When a walrus is in the water, it appears pale brown or even white. This is because blood drains from the skin's surface to stop the body losing heat. On land, the blood returns to the skin and walruses can look reddish brown or pink!

SUPERSTARDOM

Madonna, born Madonna Louise Ciecone, burst into the pop scene in 1984 with her Album Like a Virgin. She became the biggest-selling female singer in showbiz history. Her string of over 40 hits have made more than 100 million sales.

GULLIVER'S TRAVELS

The fantasy-adventure story about Gulliver in the lands of miniature people and giants, by the British author Jonathan Swift (1667–1745), is a witty satire on human foolishness. It mocks the words and deeds of politicians, scientists and philosophers.

JOKE OF THE WEEK

"What is the best time to buy a canary?"
"When it's going cheap!"

QUICK QUIZ

1. In which continent would you find alligators?
2. What type of power station splits atoms to create electricity?
3. Are all metals magnetic?
4. Who played Blackadder in the TV series?
5. How long is a regular football match?
6. What is the name of the lion in the Narnia books: Alvera, Leo, Aslan or Larry?

1. North America 2. A nuclear power station 3. No, only three 4. Rowan Atkinson 5. 90 minutes 6. Aslan

ODD ONE OUT

Which of these stands out like a sore thumb and why?

MOSCOW, MADRID, ROME, MUNICH

MUNICH – All the others are European capital cities.

May/June 2004

	school notes/homework	what's on this week
monday **31**		
tuesday **1**	Coronation of Queen Elizabeth II, 1953	
wednesday **2**		
thursday **3**		
friday **4**	The Allies liberated Rome, 1944	
saturday **5**		
sunday **6**		

FACTS OF THE WEEK

OFF INTO BATTLE

Insects have some of the best types of camouflage in the whole world of animals Shieldbugs have broad, flat bodies that look like the leaves around them. The body is shaped like the shield carried by a medieval knight-in-armour.

RADIO ENTERTAINMENT

The radio was invented by the Italian Guglielmo Marconi in 1894 at his electronics company in Chelmsford, Essex.

At first it was designed only to transmit simple messages but in 1906 music was broadcast.

COSSACK DANCER

A Cossack dancer from Ukraine leaps high in the air, showing off his agility. Cossacks were famous for their bravery and horse riding skills, and the men traditionally expressed their warlike energy in dramatic dances.

"When is an ant not an ant?"
"When it's an uncle!"

QUICK QUIZ

1. What sport are Duncan Goodhew and Mark Foster associated with?
2. Who crossed the Alps with elephants to attack Rome?
3. Complete the title of the Shakespeare play Antony and...?
4. Do cucumbers grow below or above ground?
5. What is a female lion called?
6. How much of a cake is left if you eat 4/8 of it?

1. Swimming 2. Hannibal 3. Cleopatra 4. Above ground 5. Lioness 6. Half of it

MIND PUZZLE

How many pieces are there on a chess board at the start of a game?

June 2004

	school notes/homework	what's on this week
monday **7**	Anna Kournikova, tennis player, 23 today	
tuesday **8**		
wednesday **9**		
thursday **10**	The first Oxford and Cambridge Boat Race was won by Oxford, 1829	
friday **11**	King Henry VIII married Catherine of Aragon, 1509	
saturday **12**	New Amsterdam is re-named New York, 1665	
sunday **13**		

FACTS OF THE WEEK

BABY FATHERS

Seahorse dads have the babies. They don't exactly give birth, but they store the eggs in a pouch on their belly. When the eggs are ready to hatch, a stream of miniature seahorses billows out from the dad's pouch.

SOUND RECORDINGS

The first gramophone, called a phonograph, was produced by the American inventor Thomas Alva Edison in 1878. It used cylinders to record and play sounds. Ten years later the first flat disc was introduced. A needle picked up the sound from grooves in the disc.

A MODERN SAINT?

Diana, Princess of Wales (1961-97), became famous for the work she did to help people who were ill, injured or outcast. Some people called her a 'modern saint'. But religious leaders did not approve of this title.

JOKE OF THE WEEK

"Why is the letter V like an angry bull?"
"Because it comes after U!"

QUICK QUIZ

1. How much more hydrogen than oxygen would you find in water?
2. Where would you find your Achilles tendon?
3. What letter would you add to rain to mean a railway vehicle?
4. What type of hat did Laurel and Hardy both wear?
5. What was the name of Mickey Mouse's dog?
6. With which country did Britain fight over rights to the Falkland Islands?

1. Twice as much 2. On the heel of your foot 3. T (train) 4. A bowler hat 5. Pluto 6. Argentina

ODD ONE OUT

Which of these four football grounds is the ODD ONE OUT and why?

ANFIELD, HIGHBURY, OLD TRAFFORD, IBROX

IBROX – Ibrox is in Scotland all the others are in England

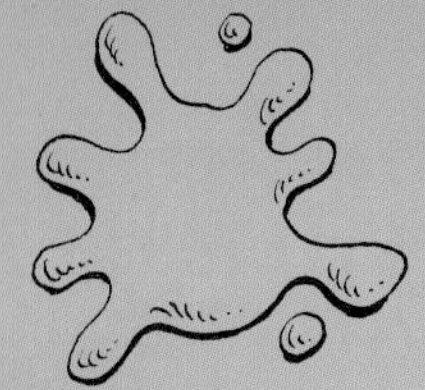

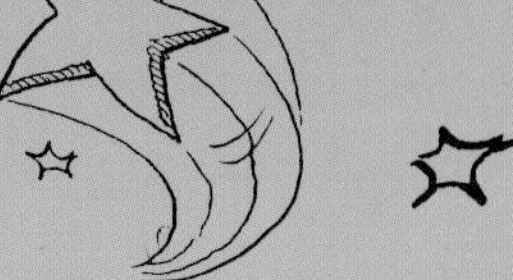

June 2004

	school notes/homework	what's on this week
monday **14**		
tuesday **15**	King John sealed the Magna Carta at Runnymede, 1215	
wednesday **16**	The first woman cosmonaut, Valentina Tereshkova, blasted off in Vostok 6, 1963	
thursday **17**	Apartheid in South Africa was ended, 1991	
friday **18**	Paul McCartney, songwriter, 62 today	
saturday **19**		
sunday **20**		

FACTS OF THE WEEK

THE EARTH IS NEARLY 5 BILLION YEARS OLD!

From a ball of molten rock Earth has changed into a living, breathing planet. We must try to keep it that way. Switching off lights to save energy and picking up litter are small things we can all do.

DINOSAUR NESTS

Like most reptiles today, dinosaurs produced young by laying eggs. These hatched out into baby dinosaurs which gradually grew into adults. Fossils have been found of eggs with dinosaurs still developing inside, as well as fossils of just-hatched baby dinosaurs.

PLAYING GOD?

Dolly the sheep was born in Scotland in 1997. Created by scientists using genetic engineering techniques, she was the first mammal to be cloned (copied) from adult cells. Some people fear that scientists are starting to copy God's role of creator.

JOKE OF THE WEEK

"Why couldn't the bike stand up by itself?"

"Because it was two tired!"

QUICK QUIZ

1. What American word is used to mean a lift?
2. What country does football star Robbie Keane come from?
3. How many dwarves featured in the story of Snow White?
4. What would you do if you 'spilled the beans'?
5. From which animal do we get the meats ham and bacon?
6. Which is the only mammal that can fly?

1. Elevator
2. Republic of Ireland 3. Seven
4. Tell or reveal the truth
5. Pig 6. The bat

WORD SEARCH

Can you find the names of five vegetables hidden below?

H	P	O	T	A	T	O	X
U	A	D	T	V	E	E	T
W	T	U	R	N	I	P	U
T	L	E	E	K	Y	R	R
J	F	L	R	O	U	H	N
S	P	I	N	A	C	H	G
S	E	F	J	R	T	N	P
C	A	R	R	O	T	Z	N

June 2004

	school notes/homework	what's on this week
monday **21**	Longest Day Prince William 22 today	
tuesday **22**	Queen Victoria celebrated her Diamond Jubilee, 1897	
wednesday **23**		
thursday **24**		
friday **25**	George Michael, singer, 41 today	
saturday **26**		
sunday **27**		

FACTS OF THE WEEK

STONE ME!

Some fish look like stones. Stone fish rest on the seabed, looking just like the rocks that surround them. If they are spotted, the poisonous spines on their backs can stun an attacker in seconds.

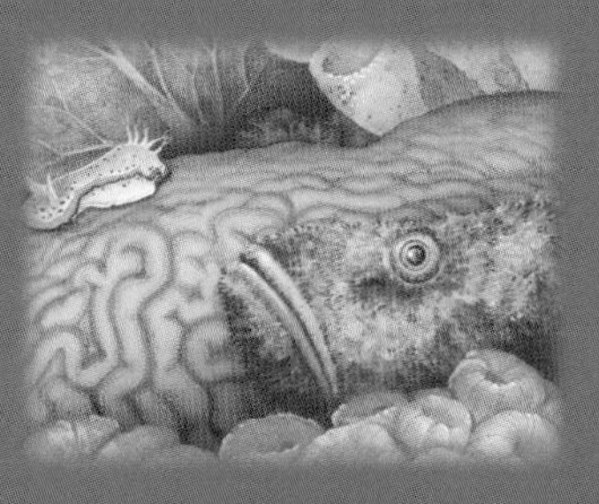

PIED PIPER

The legend of the Pied Piper tells of how, in 1284, a mysterious piper rid the town of Hamelin in Germany of its plague of rats. When the piper played his pipe, all the rats followed him to their deaths.

ESCAPOLOGIST

The Hungarian-born American Harry Houdini (1874-1926) was one of the world's greatest showmen, and the most famous 'escapologist', or escape artist. He was able to escape from chains and handcuffs while locked in a safe or immersed in a tank of water.

QUICK QUIZ

1. How many leaves does a lucky clover have?
2. Which planet is most famous for its rings?
3. How many points is the pink ball worth in snooker?
4. Which band recorded 'Yellow Submarine', 'Help' and 'A Hard Day's Night'?
5. Who explored parts of the Americas in 1492?
6. In which continent would you find llamas?

1. Four 2. Saturn 3. Six
4. The Beatles
5. Christopher Columbus
6. South America

MIND PUZZLE

How many sporting events make up a decathlon

JOKE OF THE WEEK

"What happens when you don't clean your mirror?"
"It gives you a dirty look!"

June/July 2004

	school notes/homework	what's on this week
monday **28**	The Treaty of Versailles was signed, 1919	
tuesday **29**	'The Daily Telegraph' was first published, 1855	
wednesday **30**	Tower Bridge was officially opened, 1894	
thursday **1**	Princess Diana was born 1961	
friday **2**		
saturday **3**	Tom Cruise, actor, 42 today	
sunday **4**	The Statue of Liberty was presented by France to the USA, 1883	

FACTS OF THE WEEK

KEEP WELL AWAY!

The Australian redback spider is one of the most deadly of a group called widow spiders. These spiders get their name because, once they have mated, the female may well eat the male!

CROP CIRCLES

Since the 1980s, mysterious patterns have appeared in fields of wheat in Europe and North America. Known as 'crop circles' – though they may be any shape. No one knows for certain who or what has made them – disease, jokers or even aliens!

WELL-BRED

You may be happy with your street tabby but in the cat-show world pedigrees count for everything. The forward-folded ears of this Scottish fold cat are considered a deformity in Europe, but the cat is popular in the United States.

JOKE OF THE WEEK

"What was the turtle doing on the highway?"
"About one mile per hour!"

QUICK QUIZ

1. Do olives grow under the ground, on trees or on small flowering plants?
2. Do insects have more or less legs than spiders?
3. Who is Yogi Bear's pint-sized pal?
4. What tree provides conkers in Autumn?
5. Which bird lays the largest eggs?
6. Which Hollywood film actress starred in 'Notting Hill'?

1. On trees 2. Less
3. Boo-Boo 4. Horse chestnut
5. Ostrich 6. Julia Roberts

NUMBER PUZZLE

Which number should replace the question mark?

1 3 5 7
11 13 17 19 ?
29 31 37 39 41

23 – They are all prime numbers

July 2004

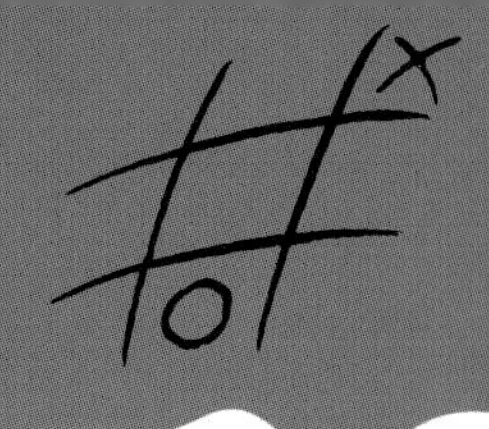

	school notes/homework	what's on this week
monday **5**	The National Health Service first started, 1948	
tuesday **6**	George W. Bush, US president, 58 today	
wednesday **7**		
thursday **8**	Tom Hanks, actor, 48 today	
friday **9**	The Battle of Britain began, 1940	
saturday **10**	Captain Cook sailed on his last voyage, 1776	
sunday **11**		

FACTS OF THE WEEK

DIVING FOR THEIR DINNER

Leatherbacks dive up to 120 metres for dinner. These turtles hold the record for being the biggest sea turtles and for making the deepest dives. Leatherbacks feed mostly on jellyfish but their diet also includes molluscs and other shellfish.

THE SPEEDY SPACE BALL

The Earth is a huge ball of rock moving through space at nearly 3000 metres per second. It weighs 6000 million, million, million tonnes. Up to two-thirds of the Earth's rocky surface is covered by water – this makes the seas and oceans. Rock that is not covered by water makes the land.

FIERY PHOENIX

The phoenix was a magical bird that lived for 500 years without eating or drinking. It lived in the deserts of the Middle East. When the time came for it to die, it set fire to itself. But it was reborn from its own ashes after three days, ready to live again.

JOKE OF THE WEEK

"Why did the spider cross the road?"
"To get to another website"!

QUICK QUIZ

1. Which character has appeared in 'The World is Not Enough' and 'Thunderball'?

2. What typical cat feature is missing from the Manx cat?

3. Who starred as both Han Solo and Indiana Jones?

4. Is the chihuahua the smallest breed of dog?

5. Which band features Bono and The Edge?

6. What is ¾ as a percentage?

1. James Bond 2. A tail 3. Harrison Ford 4. Yes 5. U2 6. 125%

WORD SEARCH

Can you find the names of five sports hidden below?

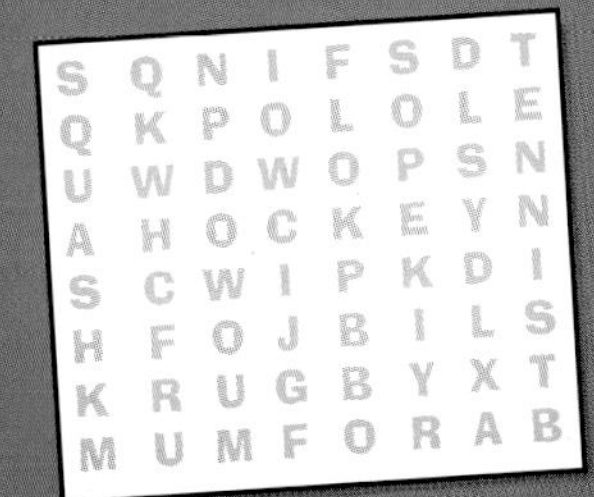

July 2004

	school notes/homework	what's on this week
monday **12**		
tuesday **13**	Harrison Ford, actor, 62 today	
wednesday **14**	The Bastille in Paris was stormed, 1789	
thursday **15**		
friday **16**	The Russian Royal Family was murdered by the Bolsheviks, 1918	
saturday **17**		
sunday **18**	Nelson Mandela, former president of South Africa, 85 today	

FACTS OF THE WEEK

THE RUIN OF ARTHUR

Lancelot was the favourite knight of King Arthur. Tales of Arthur and his Knights of the Round Table were very popular in the 1200s. Lancelot fell in love with Arthur's wife Guinevere. The struggle between the two men eventually destroyed Arthur's court.

PUNCH AND JUDY

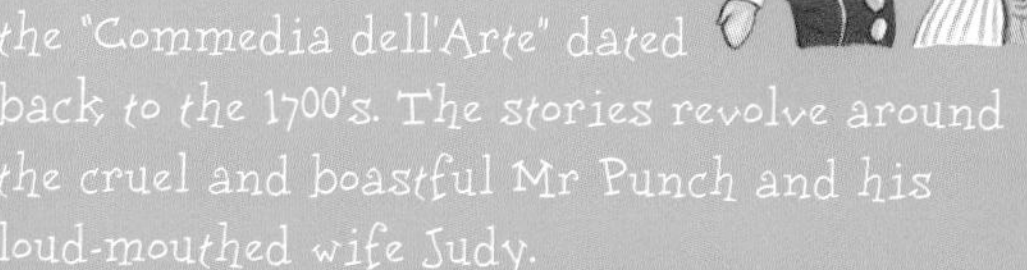

This traditional English form of puppet show, based on the old Italian farces of the "Commedia dell'Arte" dated back to the 1700's. The stories revolve around the cruel and boastful Mr Punch and his loud-mouthed wife Judy.

SPEEDY SATELLITE

TV pictures and sound can be sent rapidly around the world. They are transmitted to satellites in stationary orbit in space, and then redirected to another part of the world. This means that live news can be broadcast immediately.

JOKE OF THE WEEK

"What do you call an elephant that flies?"
"A jumbo jet!"

QUICK QUIZ

1. Which creature boasts the biggest ears in the world?
2. What fruit fell on Sir Isaac Newton's head making him consider gravity?
3. Which county does cricketer Alec Stewart play for?
4. What was the nickname given to Baron von Richthofen in World War I?
5. In which continent would you find giant pandas and the snow leopard?
6. What body in our Solar System is 330,000 times bigger than Earth?

1. African elephant
2. An apple 3. Surrey
4. The Red Baron 5. Asia
6. The Sun

ODD ONE OUT

Which of these names is the ODD ONE OUT and why?

ALEX, TIM, SAM, LOU

Tim – All the others are for both boys and girls

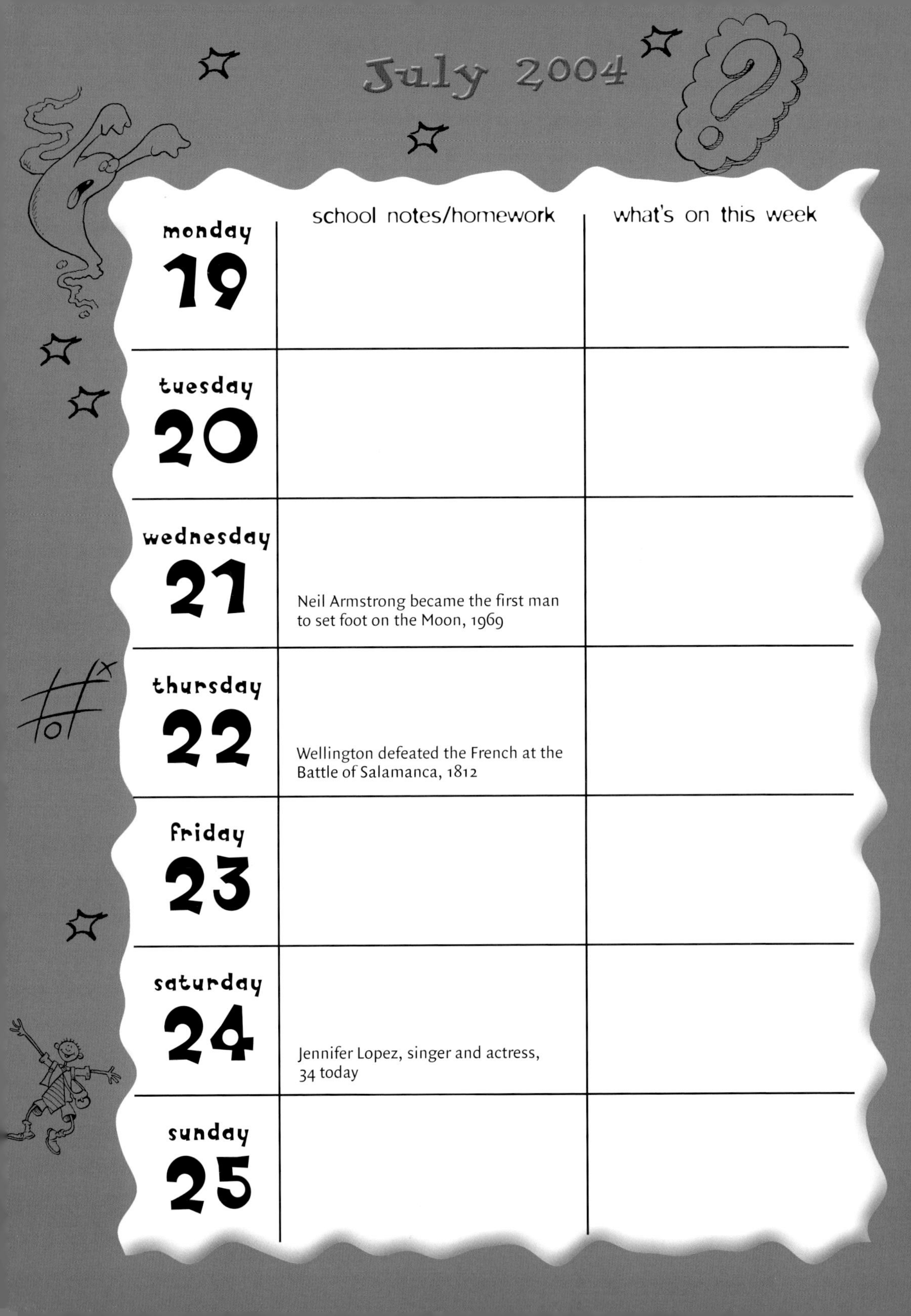

July 2004

	school notes/homework	what's on this week
monday 19		
tuesday 20		
wednesday 21	Neil Armstrong became the first man to set foot on the Moon, 1969	
thursday 22	Wellington defeated the French at the Battle of Salamanca, 1812	
friday 23		
saturday 24	Jennifer Lopez, singer and actress, 34 today	
sunday 25		

FACTS OF THE WEEK

GOING FISHING

Few creatures can survive in the dark, icy-cold ocean depths. Food is so hard to come by, the deep-sea anglerfish does not waste energy chasing prey – it has developed a clever fishing trick. A stringy 'fishing rod' with a glowing tip attracts smaller fish to the anglerfish's big mouth.

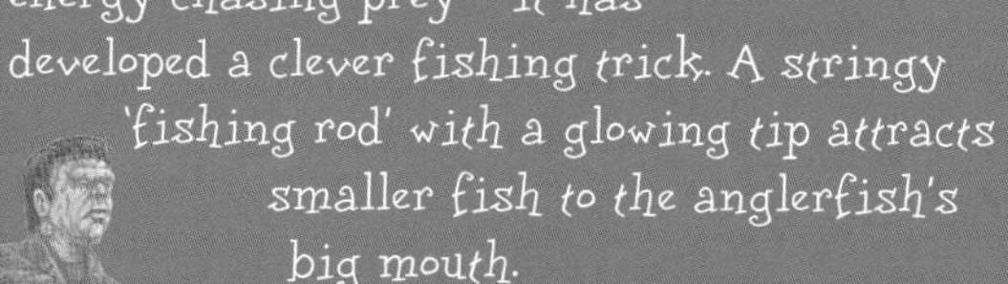

FRANKENSTEIN'S MONSTER

Created by writer Mary Shelley in 1818, Frankenstein's monster was made from dead corpses joined together. At first friendly, it turned violent and began to kill people. Frankenstein blamed himself for meddling with nature.

COLOUR WHEEL

The three primary colours are red, yellow, and blue. These can be mixed together to form orange, green and purple. On a colour wheel, one primary colour will appear opposite the mixture of the two other primary colours. These opposites are called complementary colours.

JOKE OF THE WEEK

"What do you call a spaniel dog from Spain?"
"Espaniel!"

QUICK QUIZ

1. How many degrees do the angles of a triangle add up to?
2. What kind of creatures are red admiral and cabbage white?
3. In which year did Queen Victoria die?
4. During what years did World War II take place?
5. How many feet in a yard?
6. What were Skylab and Salut early examples of?

1. 180 2. Butterflies
3. 1901 4. 1939–1945
5. 3 6. Space stations

MIND PUZZLE

How many minutes are there in five hours?

300 minutes

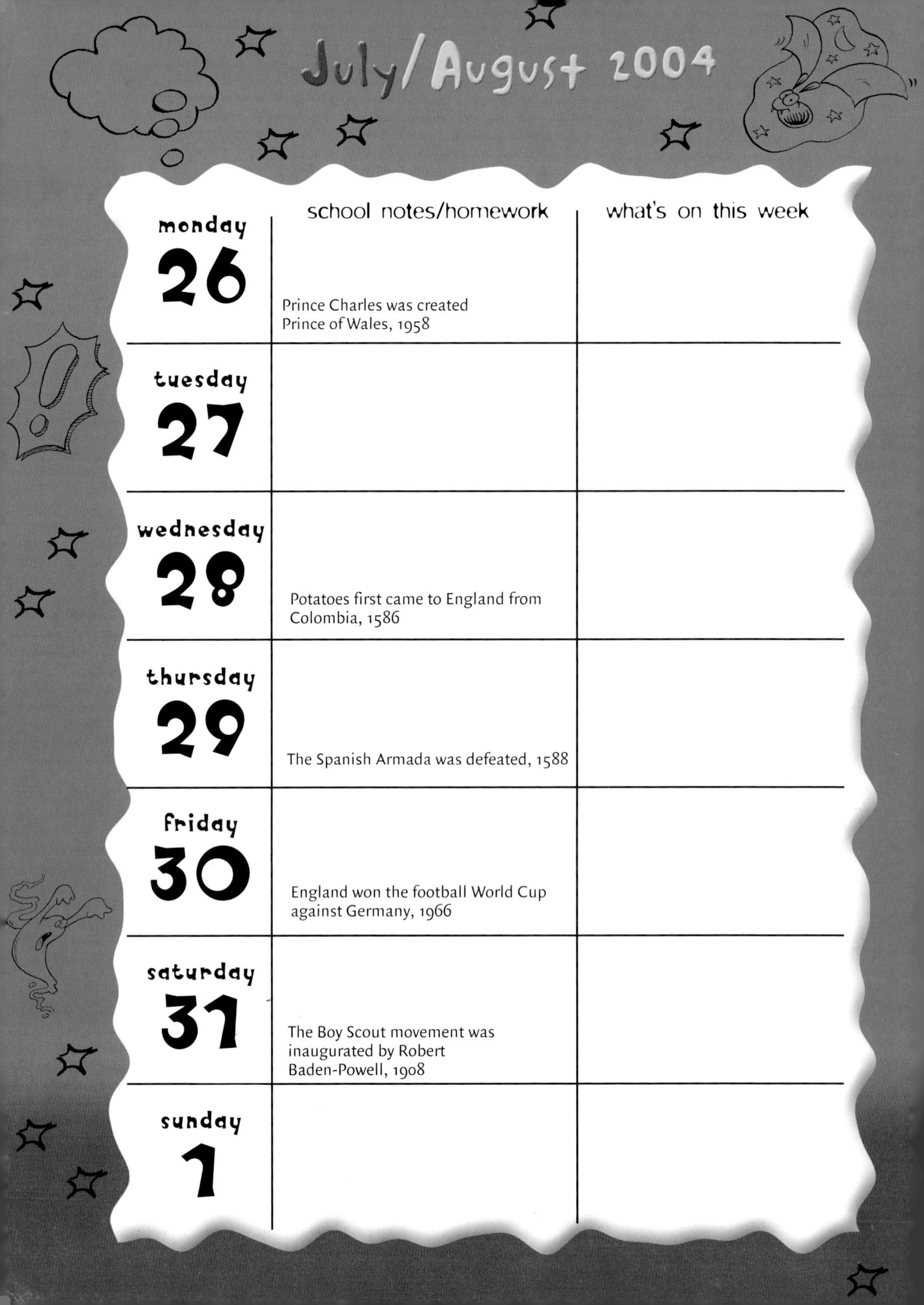

July/August 2004

	school notes/homework	what's on this week
monday 26	Prince Charles was created Prince of Wales, 1958	
tuesday 27		
wednesday 28	Potatoes first came to England from Colombia, 1586	
thursday 29	The Spanish Armada was defeated, 1588	
friday 30	England won the football World Cup against Germany, 1966	
saturday 31	The Boy Scout movement was inaugurated by Robert Baden-Powell, 1908	
sunday 1		

FACTS OF THE WEEK

DON'T FORGET THE SUNSCREEN!

Sunfish like sunbathing! Ocean sunfish are very large, broad fish that can weigh as much as 1 tonne. They are named after their habit of sunbathing on the surface of the open ocean.

BUNDLE OF FUN

Baby dinosaurs grew up to five times faster than human babies! A baby sauropod dinosaur like Diplodocus was already 1 metre long and 30 kilograms in weight when it came out of its egg!

BLOODTHIRSTY VAMPIRES

There are many stories of vampires – dead bodies that have returned to life. By day they look like ordinary people, but at night they grow wings like bats and their teeth change into fangs. The most famous vampire was Count Dracula.

JOKE OF THE WEEK

"Why do cows have bells?"
"Because their horns don't work"

1. Do wild gerbils live in deserts, forests or on the African plains?
2. Two thirds of a shark's brain is devoted to which sense?
3. What common device did Laszlo Biro of Argentina invent in 1944?
4. What is the name of the sand-filled depressions around a golf course?
5. In which country would you find Hamburg and Bremen
6. Which player moved from Leeds to Man United in the summer of 2002?

1. Deserts 2. Smell
3. The ballpoint pen (biro)
4. Bunkers 5. Germany
6. Rio Ferdinand

WORD SCRAMBLE

Unscramble the letters to find three famous English landmarks

NOTESGEHEN, GIB NEB, SELONNS NUMLOC

STONEHENGE, BIG BEN, NELSON'S COLUMN

Sports & Entertainment

TOP 10

Everyone loves making lists and we're no different. Here's some from the worlds of sport and entertainment you might find interesting

GOING FOR GOLD

Summer Olympics Medal Standings (1896–2000)

		GOLD	SILVER	BRONZE	TOTAL
1	USA	871	659	586	2116
2	USSR/Russia	498	409	371	1278
3	Germany	374	392	416	1182
4	Great Britain	180	233	225	638
5	France	188	193	217	598
6	Italy	179	143	157	479
7	Sweden	136	156	177	469
8	Hungary	150	135	158	443
9	Australia	102	110	138	350
10	Finland	101	81	114	296

CRICKET

Top international cricket teams based on number of test matches won (as of 19.11.02)

1.	AUSTRALIA	1230
2.	SOUTH AFRICA	1149
3.	PAKISTAN	1074
4.	ENGLAND	1059
5.	INDIA	1045
6.	SRI LANKA	1030
7.	NEW ZEALAND	1025
8.	WEST INDIES	996
9.	ZIMBABWE	902
10.	BANGLADESH	826

SCOTTISH FOOTBALL CLUBS

Top 5 Scottish football clubs (based on number of trophies won)

CLUB	LEAGUE	SCOT. CUP	EUROPE	LEAGUE CUP	TOTAL
1 Rangers	49	30	1	22	102
2 Celtic	38	31	1	12	82
3 Aberdeen	4	7	1	5	17
4 Hearts	4	6	0	4	14
5 Queen's Park	0	10	0	0	10

ENGLISH FOOTBALL CLUBS

Top 10 English football clubs (based on number of trophies won)

CLUB	LEAGUE	FA CUP	EUROPE	LEAGUE CUP	TOTAL
1 Liverpool	18	6	7	6	37
2 Man Utd	14	10	3	1	28
3 Arsenal	12	8	2	2	24
4 Aston Villa	7	7	1	5	20
5 Tottenham	2	8	3	3	16
6 Everton	9	5	1	0	15
7 Newcastle	5	6	1	0	12
8 Wolves	3	4	0	2	9
9 Man City	2	4	1	2	9
10 Forest	1	2	2	4	9

MOVIE MAGIC

Top 10 highest-grossing movies of all-time (based on worldwide box office receipts, $million)

1. $1835 TITANIC 1997
2. $968 HARRY POTTER & THE PHILOSOPHER'S STONE 2001
3. $925 STAR WARS: THE PHANTOM MENACE 1999
4. $920 JURASSIC PARK 1993
5. $860 LORD OF THE RINGS: FELLOWSHIP OF THE RING 2001
6. $813 INDEPENDENCE DAY
7. $798 STAR WARS: A NEW HOPE 1977
8. $791 SPIDER-MAN 2002
9. $771 THE LION KING 1994
10. $756 E.T. 1982

NUMBER ONE SINGLES

Top 10 most successful singles artistes of all-time (based on number one singles)

1. ELVIS PRESLEY (18 NUMBER ONES)
2. THE BEATLES (17)
3. CLIFF RICHARD (14)
4. WESTLIFE (11)
5. MADONNA (10)
6. ABBA (9)
7. THE SPICE GIRLS (9)
8. ROLLING STONES (8)
9. TAKE THAT (8)
10. MICHAEL JACKSON (7)

ON THE WEB

For all the latest computer games news, reviews and cheats, plus the option to play online, go to www.gameplay.com.

The World

Our planet is a pretty fascinating place, and if you don't believe us take a look at some of these stunning stats...

TOP 10 COUNTRIES BY POPULATION

1. CHINA 1.28 BILLION
2. INDIA 1.04BN
3. USA 280 MILLION
4. INDONESIA 231M
5. BRAZIL 176M
6. PAKISTAN 147M
7. RUSSIA 144M
8. BANGLADESH 133M
9. JAPAN 129M
10. NIGERIA 129M

TOP 10 MOST SPOKEN LANGUAGES

1. CHINESE MANDARIN 1.075BN
2. ENGLISH 514M
3. HINDUSTANI 496M
4. SPANISH 425M
5. RUSSIAN 275M
6. ARABIC 256M
7. BENGALI 215M
8. PORTUGUESE 194M
9. MALAY-INDONESIAN 176M
10. FRENCH 129M

TOP 10 COUNTRIES BY NUMBER OF TELEVISIONS

1. CHINA 400M
2. USA 219M
3. JAPAN 86.5M
4. INDIA 63M
5. RUSSIA 60M
6. GERMANY 51M
7. BRAZIL 36.5M
8. FRANCE 34M
9. UK 30M
10. UKRAINE 18M

TOP 10 TALLEST BUILDINGS

1. PETRONAS TOWERS, KUALA LUMPUR, 452M
2. SEARS TOWER, CHICAGO, 442M
3. JIN MAO BUILDING, SHANGHAI, 421M
4. CITIC PLAZA, GUANGZHOU, CHINA, 391M
5. SHUN HING SQUARE, SHENZOU, CHINA, 384M
6. EMPIRE STATE BUILDING, NEW YORK, 381M
7. CENTRAL PLAZA, HONG KONG, 374M
8. BANK OF CHINA TOWER, HONG KONG, 369M
9. EMIRATES TOWER NO.1, DUBAI, 355M
10. THE CENTER, HONG KONG, 350M

PHONE A FRIEND

NAME
PHONE
ADDRESS

E-MAIL

NAME
PHONE
ADDRESS

E-MAIL

NAME
PHONE
ADDRESS

E-MAIL

NAME
PHONE
ADDRESS

E-MAIL

NAME
PHONE
ADDRESS

E-MAIL

NAME
PHONE
ADDRESS

E-MAIL

NAME
PHONE
ADDRESS

E-MAIL

NAME
PHONE
ADDRESS

E-MAIL

NAME
PHONE
ADDRESS

E-MAIL

NAME
PHONE
ADDRESS

E-MAIL

NAME
PHONE
ADDRESS
E-MAIL

NAME
PHONE
ADDRESS
E-MAIL

NAME
PHONE
ADDRESS
E-MAIL

NAME
PHONE
ADDRESS
E-MAIL

NAME
PHONE
ADDRESS
E-MAIL

NAME
PHONE
ADDRESS
E-MAIL

NAME
PHONE
ADDRESS
E-MAIL

NAME
PHONE
ADDRESS
E-MAIL

NAME
PHONE
ADDRESS
E-MAIL

NAME
PHONE
ADDRESS
E-MAIL

PHONE A FRIEND

NAME
PHONE
ADDRESS
E-MAIL

NAME
PHONE
ADDRESS
E-MAIL

NAME
PHONE
ADDRESS
E-MAIL

NAME
PHONE
ADDRESS
E-MAIL

NAME
PHONE
ADDRESS
E-MAIL

NAME
PHONE
ADDRESS
E-MAIL

NAME
PHONE
ADDRESS
E-MAIL

NAME
PHONE
ADDRESS
E-MAIL

NAME
PHONE
ADDRESS
E-MAIL

NAME
PHONE
ADDRESS
E-MAIL

NAME ______________________

PHONE ______________________

ADDRESS ______________________

____

____

E-MAIL ______________________

NAME ______________________

PHONE ______________________

ADDRESS ______________________

____

____

E-MAIL ______________________

NAME ______________________

PHONE ______________________

ADDRESS ______________________

____

____

E-MAIL ______________________

NAME ______________________

PHONE ______________________

ADDRESS ______________________

____

____

E-MAIL ______________________

NAME ______________________

PHONE ______________________

ADDRESS ______________________

____

____

E-MAIL ______________________

NAME ______________________

PHONE ______________________

ADDRESS ______________________

____

____

E-MAIL ______________________

NAME ______________________

PHONE ______________________

ADDRESS ______________________

____

____

E-MAIL ______________________

NAME ______________________

PHONE ______________________

ADDRESS ______________________

____

____

E-MAIL ______________________

NAME ______________________

PHONE ______________________

ADDRESS ______________________

____

____

E-MAIL ______________________

NAME ______________________

PHONE ______________________

ADDRESS ______________________

____

____

E-MAIL ______________________

First published by Bardfield Press in 2003

Bardfield Press is an imprint of
Miles Kelly Publishing Ltd
Bardfield Centre, Great Bardfield, Essex CM7 4SL

2 4 6 8 10 9 7 5 3 1

Project Management
Ruthie Boardman

Design
Michelle Cannatella, Maya Currell, Andy Knight, Debbie Meekcoms

Editorial Director
Anne Marshall

Picture Research
Liberty Newton

Production
Estela Godoy

British Library Cataloguing-in-Publication Data
A catalogue record for this book is available from the British Library

ISBN 1-84236-252-6

Printed in China

The publishers wish to thank the following artists who have contributed to this book:
Andy Beckett (Linden Artists), Dave Burrows, Jim Channell,
Kuo Kang Chen, Mark Davies, Peter Dennis, Richard Draper,
Wayne Ford, Terry Gabbey, Luigi Galante, Alan Hancocks,
Sally Holmes, Richard Hook (Linden Artists), Rob Jakeway,
John James (Temple Rogers), Steve Kirk, Mick Loates (Linden Artists)
Andy Lloyd Jones, Kevin Maddison, Alan Male, Janos Marffy,
Massimiliano Maugeri (Galante Studios), Angus McBride,
Doreen McGuinness, Andrea Morandi, Tracey Morgan, Steve Roberts
Martin Sanders, Peter Sarson, Rob Sheffield, Ted Smart, Nick Spender
Roger Stewart, Gwen Touret, Rudi Vizi, Christian Webb
Steve Weston, Mike White (Temple Rogers)

The publishers wish to thank the following sources for the photographs used in this book:
Buena vista/Walt Disney/Pictorial Press; Pictorial Press
All other pictures from Corel, Digital STOCK, Dover Publications, Hemera, ILN
The publishers would like to thank Great Bardfield Primary School for their advice.

e-mail: info@mileskelly.net

www.mileskelly.net